veterinary Hospital

LOVE, Jo :)

The
Name Game

A6

The
Name Game

An Eclectic Look at How and Why
People Name Their Pets

Wendy Nan Rees

Photos by Dot Stovall

 Howell Book House
New York

Howell Book House
A Simon & Schuster Macmillan Company
1633 Broadway
New York, NY 10019-6785

Macmillan is a registered trademark of Macmillan, Inc.

Library of Congress Cataloging-in-Publication Data

Rees, Wendy Nan.

The name game : an eclectic look at how and why people name their pets / Wendy Nan Rees : photos by Dot Stovall.

p. cm.

ISBN 0-87605-693-1

1. Pets—Names. 2. Pets—Anecdotes. I. Stovall, Dot.
II. Title.
SF411.3.R44 1996   96-10843
929.9'7—dc20   CIP

DESIGN BY GEORGE J. McKEON

Manufactured in the United States of America.
10 9 8 7 6 5 4 3 2 1

Contents

Acknowledgments

I want to thank all of the generous people who have been involved with this project. It has truly been a labor of love and without you this never could have come to light.

Special thanks to Felice Primeau and Ariel Cannon, my editors, for taking our endless phone calls. You were always there and have given us invaluable direction.

Dot Stovall, you gave so much of yourself. Thank you! We could not have done it without you. We had a blast!

More thanks and kudos to Carol Blinken Emquies (you are special, sister), Larry Turner, Esq. (for keeping it all together), Susan Dubow (your timing was always right on), Gina Rugolo, Julie Silverman (and Tammy), Jana Howington (for sharing S.L.), Paul Kaplan, Kathy Kaehler, Billy Koch, Loris Kramer, Steve Wilson, Suzie Fairchild (Ace pinch hitter), Clive (for all your computer help), Don Weinstein and Photo Impact in L.A., and last, but definitely not least, Sunrise 24-Hour Direct Delivery Service.

Finally, thanks to Webster and Stella Bella—whose names inspired this book.

Dedication

I have two very special people in my life to whom I would like to dedicate this book.

First, to my husband, Tom Rees, thank you for your unconditional love and support. I feel so blessed to have a husband and friend like you. I love you!

Second, to my good friend and partner, Steve LuKanic (who has had the summer of his life!). Not a day went by when you weren't here, holding up the fort, keeping track of all the people, pets and places. Your help is so greatly appreciated, and so is your friendship. It is one I cherish.

To both of these men, thank you. This book could not have happened without you.

xoxo

Wendy

About the Author

Since she was two years old, Wendy Nan Rees has loved animals. Her first pets were an English Setter named Digby and a pony named Ricky, and over the years she's grown attached to many dogs, cats, horses, and just about everything else. Her love of animals and her concern for their well-being have led Wendy to become an entrepreneur and author. She is the creator of Lip Smackers, a company dedicated to providing healthy, all-natural treats for pets, and her cookbooks for pets, *No Barking at the Table* and *No Catnapping in the Kitchen*, will be published by Howell Book House this year. Wendy lives in Los Angeles with her husband Tom and her two best friends, Webster and Stella Bella.

About the Photographer

Dot Stovall is a freelance photographer who lives in Los Angeles with her favorite subjects: her two cats, Opie and Otis, and her dog, Daisy. Dot continues to photograph them, along with anything or anyone else that catches her eye and heart.

PAWS/LA

Part of the proceeds from this book will go to the charity PAWS/LA. I chose PAWS because this wonderful organization not only helps animals, it helps people. People and their pets share such a unique and strong bond, and this organization works to preserve that bond when it is needed most. The work PAWS is doing is extraordinary, and I applaud their efforts.

PAWS/LA was started in 1989 by a handful of concerned people who saw a need to assist people living with AIDS in the care of their pets. We've grown from six clients in 1989 to 875 clients today. Those concerned about the quality of life of people living with AIDS have helped to ensure that the much-needed, unconditional love of pets remains a part of life. There are now almost 30 organizations nationwide doing similar work for people living with AIDS.

Our ability to provide pet food, vet care, dog-walking and other services is due to the hundreds of generous donors and volunteers who allow the organization to continue. Thank you for your support of this exciting and generous project, and for your support of PAWS/LA.

Nadia Sutton
EXECUTIVE DIRECTOR

Steve Wayland
ADMINISTRATOR

Joel Kimmel
DEVELOPMENT DIRECTOR

Introduction

Name \nam\ n 1 a: a word or phrase that constitutes the distinctive designation of a person, pet or thing.

Okay, so I added "pet" to the above definition from *Webster's New Collegiate Dictionary*—but that's only because our pets' names are just as important as our own.

Have you ever asked a person their middle name, and they won't tell you because they hate it? Think for a moment how our beloved pets would react to a name *they* didn't like. Would they mope around, bark, meow, whinny…run away? Of course not. Our pets give us unconditional love, and they don't know what's in a name. But there are limitations! You wouldn't want to name your pet "Sit" or "Stay," because that could cause a great deal of confusion. Also, know that at some point in time, you'll have to yell your pet's name across a street or park, and you wouldn't want to yell an ugly or rude name. Imagine the looks you'd get.

So how do you begin to name a pet? Like a newborn baby, you haven't spent much time with it, so you really don't know its personality or characteristics. In fact, other than looks, you really don't have much to go on…

The idea for this book came to me one night at a large family gathering. At the time, I was thinking about getting a third dog (an English Bull Mastiff). Wondering out loud what a good name for such a large, distinctive dog would be, something unexpected happened. They went mad! Names started to flow…Tank, Lance, Mac, Bennie, Coach, Caesar, Napoleon, Butch, Tiny, Trojan, Natrone, Emmit, Troy, Reggie, Big Frank, O.J. (no comment), Dexter, Bruce, Mufaasa, Scar, Leonard, Bettis, Jerome, Bennett, Doc, Lou Holtz, Dino, Tiwy, Hank, Salmon, Tuna, Grampa, Slip, Marco Polo and Fido. As a "want-to-be" history buff and Anlgophile, I personally thought a name with the ring of nobility would be fun…Ambassador, Baron, Count, Duke, Earl, Major, Prince, King, Bishop, Emperor, General, Yeoman. You get the idea.

The conversation eventually shifted, and people began telling their favorite stories behind how and why they named *their* dogs, cats, birds, horses, etc. At that moment, the idea for this book was born.

In preparation, I started off by asking my family and friends how and why they named their pets. That led to them asking *their* families and friends the same question…and so on…and so on…and so on!

In the course of putting this book together, I have been amazed at how much love and energy people put forth when it comes to their extended animal family. To pet lovers, very little else in life matters more than their dear animals. I have tried to capture that love and energy in the pages that follow.

In this book, you will meet over 100 people and their pets from all walks of life—from the "rich and famous in Hollywood" to the "family next door." Each and every one of them has a unique story to tell about the special animal in their lives. And when it comes to the pets themselves, while dogs are obviously a mainstay, many other wonderful (and sometimes unique) animals are also favorites.

The last section in this book includes a list of names to help those readers who may be struggling to find the perfect name for that new family member. Whether it's a dog, cat, fish, rabbit, pig or any other domesticated (or not!) animal, this list and the stories of the pet lovers that follow should help get your imagination warmed up!

Part 1

The
Name Game

Wendy Nan & Tom Rees and WEBSTER & STELLA

My first dog, Webster, received his name in a huge rush. He arrived at six weeks old and was covered in so many wrinkles he could hardly walk (he's a Shar-Pei). It was very close to the deadline for sending in his registration papers, and on top of that, the breeder was going out of town. She asked me if I had a name picked out, or if I could at least name him while she waited on the phone. How on earth was I going to name this puppy in three minutes?

Looking around the room, I spotted a copy of *Webster's Dictionary* on my bookshelf. In my mind I hoped this puppy would turn out to be a sweet, loving, extremely smart dog. Well, Webster seemed perfect! Hence, my dog was to be named after the "Great Book." That was ten years ago. Then came my second dog, Stella. Webster was getting old and not moving around much. The vet suggested that a female puppy would give him new life, the idea being the more he moved, the less stiff he would be from arthritis. I wasn't really thrilled with the idea of a second puppy. The thought of crate training, sleepless nights, accidents on my carpet, and all the problems associated with puppyhood scared me. But I was ready to do anything for Webster, so I went on a hunt for a breeder of French Bulldogs.

It took six months of looking for just the right puppy. One evening in late September 1992, a breeder called and told me about a batch of six rescued "Frenchies" from Santa Barbara that she'd had for a month. She felt there was one who had the personality to hold her own in my house, and this puppy loved being around people and dogs. I was eating dinner at the time, and I looked over at my friend Tim and said, "What a great thing…not only could I get the dog I wanted, but she'd be rescued from a bad home."

The breeder gave me all the specs on the dog. She was a six-month-old Frenchie. Her color was Brindle (black, white and brown), with three white paws and a pink-and-white chest. The breeder asked if we could come over right away. Of course we would, and my last question was, "What's her name?" She answered…"BUBBLES."

As we rushed to the car, Tim asked if the puppy had a name. I nodded. He looked at me…"So, what is it?" I couldn't hold back…"Bubbles!" The expression on his face was priceless, and we both burst out laughing.

When we arrived at the breeder's, twenty French Bulldogs of all shapes and sizes greeted us at the door. Tim wanted to run, but Bubbles ran right to him. At that moment, both the breeder and I knew we'd be taking the puppy home.

We spent two hours there, and yes, Bubbles did come home with us that night. As we were driving home, we pondered names aloud. I thought she looked like "Yoda," (from *Star Wars*) but Tim felt she had the personality and looks of a "Stella Dora" (meaning "gold star"). Okay, I liked Stella, but not Dora, so we thought about it for a few minutes and came up with Stella Bella. Bella means beautiful in Italian—not exactly the description that most people would link with a French Bulldog, but she is beautiful to us and always will be!

—Wendy Nan Rees

A special note: On July 11, 1996, Webster passed away at the age of twelve. He was my best friend and his name will live on forever. He will be greatly missed. Good-bye old friend. I love you.

—Wendy

Sally Harvey and TAOS

*I*t was August 1986, and I was moving across the country to California in a fully packed car. When we stopped at an Indian pueblo in Taos, New Mexico, this starving puppy ran up to us like we had just arrived home after a long trip. The pack of mangy dogs he was with ran away when he tried to join them, so the puppy followed us and we bought him some bread from an outdoor oven. After a while my friend asked if we should take him with us. I thought it was a good idea. I asked two Native Americans sitting on a porch across the river what the story was. "They're all strays around here," they said. "No one wants them." As we got ready to leave, I opened the car door and the puppy jumped right in. Later that night I saw a coyote on the side of the road looking back over his shoulder like a hitchhiker, watching as we passed. Taos was asleep on my lap; he was magical and safe, and stayed that way.

—Sally Harvey

Miles & Anabella and OUTLAW

My name is Miles and I have a special bunny named Outlaw. She got her name because she's wild and she doesn't follow anyone's law but her own. Everyday, I invite my girlfriend, Anabella, over to play with me and Outlaw, and it's always fun because we pretend we're outlaws, too. Sometimes we even dress up like we're in the Wild West and we crawl after Outlaw the bunny as she hops around the garden. Then we usually go back inside, eat some cookies with milk, and take a long nap.

—Miles

LaTonya, Samuel & Zoe Jackson and SMITHEE

Our dog, Smithfield Christian Jackson, was a graduation gift to our daughter, Zoe—one which she begged for and which Sam begged me not to give. Although Sam is known for his work in the movies, my background is really in the theater—and in the theater, everyone's dog has a great name. This little European Scottie looked like a ham—a Smithfield ham, so we named him Smithfield! His middle name, Christian, was just a way of elongating the name, and since *we're* Christian, we figured we'd give him a religious "christening" too. Of course, usually we just call him Smithee.

—LaTonya Jackson

Marta Kauffman and COUGAR

Unless you are at a certain stage in your riding, you don't get horses as babies—you can't very well go to the ASPCA, pick up a horse and name it whatever you want. So, when I went to look at my horse for the first time, his barn name was already Cougar—which we chose to keep just because it was so darn cute. But his show name was Noble Spirit, which I found a little pretentious. Well, my daughter heard me talking on the phone as I was in the process of buying him, saying to a friend of mine that I thought buying this horse was just a bit of "middle-age madness." So that became his show name!

We also have another horse, Toto; a standard poodle named Otis, who's just the prince of all dogs; three cats: Martini, Leonard and Gus; a dwarf hamster named Chubby Cheeks; and an aquarium filled with fish that my son has named after all the superheroes.

—Marta Kauffman

Michael Kaplan and DIANE

I purchased two iguanas in 1991. I bought two instead of one because, let's face it, you can never have too many iguanas around. As far as cold-blooded reptiles go, they're really quite lovable.

By profession I'm a writer for television, and I also happen to be an avid viewer. This helps explain why I chose to name my two baby lizards Sam and Diane, after the characters from *Cheers*.

The unfortunate irony is that my iguanas had a relationship that closely resembled that of the characters they were named after. At first, they were congenial at the water bowl and down-right polite around the spinach and kale. This behavior quickly gave way to squabbling and tension which made the terrarium an unpleasant place for everyone.

In the end I had to give Sam away to another iguana lover (I wanted to make sure he wouldn't

wind up a pair of boots). Although *I* still miss Sam on occasion, Diane seems to have adjusted well to the life of a single lizard in the 90s. She is currently enjoying her lifestyle of eating, sleeping and pooping.

—Michael Kaplan

Robyn Kreger and
BRITAIN VALENTINE

Britain (named after England, a country I became fascinated with at ten years old after seeing the film *Mary Poppins*—still one of my favorites!) Valentine (because everyone should have a middle name, and she was born on Valentine's Day!) is crazy about tuna fish, loves to drink from the bathtub spigot, and has occasionally been known to fetch. Her favorite channel is MTV, her favorite movie is *Grease* (don't even try to tear her away during the final dance number—even with a can of tuna), and she loves to sit right next to the speakers when the CD player is on. This cat loves music!

—Robyn Kreger

Stefanie, Nannie & George Wilson and JESSIE

We got Jessie through a business deal. We made the deal, she gave us the business. Actually, she's the sweetest dog in the world. Even though she's big, she's the gentlest creature. When our daughter, Nannie, was a baby, Jessie would stand guard, literally patroling the perimeter.

Anyway, we got her through this real estate transaction my husband, David, and his brother were working on. They told the principal they were looking for a dog, and the guy sent them down to his warehouse where the foreman had Jessie in back. It was love at first bark.

How did Jessie get her name? Well, we have a friend who has a dog (who's actually a wolf) named Jessie. Nannie and our son, George, had never seen such a big dog. Georgie thought it was a horse. Anyway, this wolf-dog is so well trained, we thought maybe some of that would rub off on our dog. So we named her Jessie, too. Of course, in retrospect, obedience school probably would have been the smarter plan.

—Stefanie Wilson

Warren Eckstein and RIO

My dog, Rio, was "the next hello" after losing my beloved Tigo, the "Buster Brown" dog who gave me fifteen years of companionship. Prior to our introduction, the first eight months of Rio's life were traumatic. He had been shuttled through three different homes and had an appointment to be destroyed when the Seattle Shepherd Rescue group saved him. When I saw him, I immediately recognized the distinct and impressive championship line he was undoubtedly bred from. "How did he get here?" was a question most people would ask, but irresponsible pet owners don't just own "generic" dogs. I also rescued him from his previous name—Barney! Four years later, he's still enjoying his delayed puppyhood, with every new toy on the market!

—Warren Eckstein

Will & Judith Bright and SAM

Someone had given us this overgrown cat they couldn't keep any longer. We couldn't think of a name for him, so one night we were sitting on the couch watching *Cheers*. After trying different names like Larry, Bob, and Ralph, we sat there watching "Sam Malone" and decided Sam was the perfect name for this cat.

We also have two other cats. Eve was also given to us by someone who couldn't take care of her. She's all black, and we got her on Halloween—All Hallow's "Eve"—so naming her was easy. And as for Molly, our third cat—we wanted a marmalade kitty, so we picked the runt of a litter and named her something Irish to match her red coloring.

—Will & Judith Bright

Malcolm-Jamal Warner
and MECCA & MAKEBA

My Pit Bull's name is Mecca after the holy place in the Middle East. The word is also slang for "the greatest"—and this dog is! My Rottweiler, Makeba, is named after Miriam Makeba, a South African singer and political activist.

The dogs are good pals and get along great. I brought Mecca home when she was six weeks old, so she's like Makeba's daughter now. You can't look at Mecca wrong, or you're in trouble with Makeba!

For now, I've pretty much got my hands full with these two. I always tell my friends, whenever you even begin to *think* about having kids—get a dog first!

—Malcolm-Jamal Warner

14

Sally & James Wilson and TUCKER

We got Tucker from a friend who found him running down a busy street. James and I picked him up and we named him Tucker. Now, the story we tell for public consumption is that we named him after James' sister's son, a cool little blond-haired boy named, obviously, Tucker. But the real reason is quite different.

You see, I'm from England, where we have this thing called "cockney rhyming slang." Instead of using a vulgarity, we use a word that rhymes with it. And then, to make it even less offensive, we use a word associated with the rhyme, and that becomes the substitute for the vulgarity. Here's an example: a "raspberry"—the kind you hear at a ball game—is called a raspberry because raspberry is associated with "tart," as in raspberry tart. And tart rhymes with…well, you know.

To make a long story short, we noticed from the beginning that Tucker was going to be a handful, to put it nicely. So, if you extrapolate from the above, you'll figure out how we came to name him Tucker.

—Sally Wilson

Mary Park and RACHEL

Rachel's given name is Jamboree "Regan" Rumbosa, but I discovered soon after this adorable Wheaten Terrier got off the plane that her kennel name just didn't fit. She had such a sweet, lovable face—I wanted her to have a name to match. I tried to think of something that sounded close to Regan (since that was what she was used to)—and "Rachel" came to mind.

Rachel and I are inseparable now, and she's become a genuine party dog; as a party and event coordinator for the last 25 years, I've thrown all her birthday parties! Her first party was "Bows and Ties" (which she wore). Birthday #2 had a rodeo theme, and Rachel looked like the perfect cowgirl. For her third birthday, I threw her a "Doggietaunte Ball" (her coming-out party); her fourth was "Le Cirque de Chien" (a real doggie circus); and her fifth was a gala Hawaiian Luau, complete with grass skirts and leis.

It brings me great joy to plan her parties, and in lieu of gifts, Rachel asks for donations to PAWS/LA and and other charities. At each party she has raised close to $2500!

—Mary Park

Belle

At first I wanted a ferret, but since they eat crops and are illegal in the state of California, a pet store owner recommended a pot belly pig instead. Initially I laughed at the thought of owning a farmyard animal, but I was interested enough to check out the one arriving in the store the following week. My partner, Jim, and I went back to the store to spend time with the piglet and fell in love with her. (Well, I fell in love—Jim needed persuading). A few weeks later, through a breeder in Missouri, we adopted a little black one. At the time she joined our family, the Disney version of *Beauty and the Beast* was released. Well, she was a beauty, so we named her Belle. She's sweet and affectionate—sometimes a pain in the ass—but we love her madly!

Bugsy (Bugs)

It was time for a second pet, although Jim needed persuading. I thought perhaps this time we should get a traditional animal—maybe a dog. I always liked the look of a Shar-Pei, and after reading up on them I was convinced this was the breed. Playful, smart, loyal and loving, not to mention that a Shar-Pei could pass as Belle's sibling. We picked ours out of many litters strictly based on appearance and personality. In the first few weeks of living with us she had several names: Roxie, Sable and Garbo to name a few. But she finally became Bugsy (a.k.a. Bugs) because her face looks like a gangster's and she carries dog bones in her mouth like cigars.

At this time, I'd like a third pet—possibly a French Bulldog. But Jim needs persuading.

—John Begly

17

James Allen and ONE-FISH, TWO-FISH, DR. SEUSS & DOROTHY PARKER

One day we were having Dim Sum in Chinatown. My son, James, is very outgoing and became fast friends with the waiters, who delighted in holding him over the fish tanks to observe the various sea creatures up close. As I watched them I thought, "Isn't that cute" and then, "If they drop my son in that tank they're dead." When we left the restaurant, one of the waiters presented James with a beautiful red shrimp in a plastic bag filled with water. Well, I knew we couldn't keep the shrimp. Sure, it might be delicious lightly breaded and fried in olive oil and garlic, but I didn't think my son would appreciate that. More importantly, the shrimp would need saltwater to survive and couldn't live with James' freshwater goldfish, One-Fish and Two-Fish, that he already had at home. So we proceded directly to a pet store where the owner made us a trade: our new saltwater shrimp for two rather innocuous, pale *freshwater* shrimp. It was the perfect solution. We brought them home, introduced them to the goldfish, and named them after our favorite authors, Dr. Seuss and Dorothy Parker.

—Lisa & James Allen

Rosanna Arquette and BISOU

First I had a Lhasa Apso named Lulu. She was the love of my life, and I took her everywhere with me. Then one horrible night, she got killed by a coyote. I was so upset—I couldn't believe she was gone. What made it worse was I had to go to the Cannes Film Festival that week, and since the French really like dogs, I had planned to bring her with me. During my whole time in Cannes, I was so depressed—people even tried giving me puppies to take back to America, but knowing they'd have to sit in quarantine forever, I just couldn't accept. When I got back a friend of mine took me to a breeder. She thought I should get another Lhasa Apso "immediately." So I did— a cute little Lhasa Apso puppy, six weeks old, who ran into my arms the minute I saw her. She was so tiny, and so cute and funny. She was supposed to be red in color, but the strange thing is she *never* turned red. She became white and eventually looked exactly like Lulu! (Sometimes I think she *is* Lulu.) It didn't take long to fall in love with this puppy—she took baths with me, she slept with me. And she would do this thing where she'd get on her hind legs and dance. It was hysterical. I named her Bisou because I lived in Paris for awhile and people there always say, "Bisou, Bisou!" (or "Kiss, Kiss!"). I always loved that word, and I thought it was a great name for a dog. And since Bisou loves to give me kisses—it's perfect!

—Rosanna Arquette

Roy Wood and BOB

My pets have always been the type that *eat* the furry, cute, cuddly and adorable critters you find wagging their tales or purring in the family room. They may not "love you back" like Fluffy or Spot, but who needs love when you have your very own Discovery Channel episode every time they eat? (Kal Kan kind of pales in comparison.)

I named my Spectacled Caimen alligator Bob after Bobby Collins, an alligator trapper in Florida. I was filming a documentary on Bobby, so I bought Bob.

Bobby may not agree, but I think they look alike.

—Roy Wood

Robby Koch and TABITHA, JESSIE & OZZIE

I first got my little princess Jessie, a Border Collie and Australian Shepherd mix, when I was three. I took a trip to the Amanda Foundation with my family to pick out a dog and when I saw Jessie I knew she was perfect for us. The act of naming Jessie was a big misunderstanding, though. I wanted to name the dog Chelsey, but because I was very young and still not speaking clearly, my family thought I was saying "Jessie." So the name stuck.

Ozzie, my German Shepherd, was named after the St. Louis Cardinals' shortstop Ozzie Smith. He was my brother's favorite baseball player which, of course, also made him mine. Ironically, they have some very similar characteristics: both Ozzies are very gentle souls who would do anything for their masters, or in Smith's case, his team.

Tabitha, the newest member of our family, was named after the daughter in the TV series *Bewitched*. I got her a couple of weeks before the Los Angeles earthquake in January of 94. She ended sleeping through the entire quake which made us think she was a little mysterious, or maybe just really tired.

I'll always love my dogs. They're there when you need a friend, and they never talk back.

—Robby Koch

Deirdre de'Tappan & Dennis Kwiecinski and MAX

Ode to Max

"That comes to $1200. Cash or credit?"

The salesman baited us with "You won't regret it!"

For the dog, the insurance, the miscellaneous fees,

Not to mention those pricey accessories.

But it was Christmas…

A poor time for a budget.

Over the budget—now that had a ring to it.

Even better, the name "Max" seemed appropriate.

Since then a mortgage (a house with a yard),

A seven-foot fence and a four-door car.

All for our dog.

Max is the ultimate!

—Deirdre de'Tappan & Dennis Kwiecinski

Paula & Lewis Turner and Friends

When Lewis first became aware of the world of parrots, he knew that at some point in his life he would spend time with the magnificent Hyacinth Macaw. The Hyacinth is the largest of all macaws and the parrot family. They are rare and are slaughtered in their homeland for their brilliant cobalt blue feathers.

Lewis's opportunity came with the opening of his first pet store. He researched and found the best breeder who introduced him to this beautiful bird, hand-fed for over one year, adorable…and HUGE!

The intent was for the Hyacinth to live at the store on a tree made especially for him, occasionally travelling with us as we appeared as guests on various TV shows describing the innovative concept of the pet store. (One of the purposes for getting a Hyacinth was to be able to inform the public about their plight and demonstrate the differences between domestic hand-fed birds and imported ones.)

We decided both the staff and customers should participate in naming our new "mascot," so we initiated the "Name Our Store Pet Contest." We received hundreds of entries and it was tough to choose the winner, but we finally chose "Bixby." We were quite pleased with the choice, especially since we had always admired the actor Bill Bixby who had passed away only a few months earlier.

For a good part of Lewis's life, he has practiced the art of prestidigitation (a fancy name for magic) and he's kept on practicing each trick until he got it right. Of all the rabbits assisting him with his acts, the two that stand out most are a Polish dwarf named Mikey and a Holland Lop named Whiskers.

The name "Mikey" was inspired by the successful cereal commercial on TV at the time—the one where the two older brothers wouldn't eat the cereal because it was supposed to be "good for them," so they passed the box to their little brother, saying "Hey, let's get Mikey…he won't eat it, he hates everything!" Well, the "Mikey" in the commercial had the same adorable personality as our little "rabbette" (baby rabbit), so the name was perfect. The story behind Whiskers is not quite as elaborate. As a "rabbette," his nose and whiskers moved constantly, even when he was sleeping, so Whiskers just seemed like the appropriate name for this guy.

Throughout his magic career Lewis also worked with many doves, but he never really developed a bonding relationship with any of them—until Precious became part of the family. This snowflake-white bird became an appendage to me, and I poured so much love into him that Precious did things Lewis was never able to get a dove to do. Now Precious follows me from room to room and will come to me whenever I call him. His favorite pastime is sitting on top of the bathroom door while I'm doing my morning routine. (He does other sorts of manly things on my leg, but that's another story…)

We acquired our cat, Peepers, from a breeder when he was about eight weeks old, and we immediately fell in love with him—especially how he looked at us with his big eyes. One evening, as Lewis was playing with this still unnamed kitten, he asked, "How did you get those enormous peepers?" And the rest is history.

—Paula Turner

Phil McKenna & Ruben Gonzalez and HUBBELL

We never planned to get a puppy. All we planned was a relaxing weekend retreat with friends, unaware that my best friend, Jeff, had an ulterior motive. Jeff's Cocker Spaniels, Ricky and Lucy, had just had a litter of puppies six weeks earlier. They were all cute, but one truly stood out from the rest. He was white and tan with freckles on his nose and the longest eyelashes I'd ever seen. Although Jeff originally planned to keep him, he decided the three dogs he already had were enough. That's when his plot began. Jeff was sure that a weekend with the puppy would leave me and my roommate, Ruben, begging to keep him. But after going back and forth with our decision, we decided against it. Jeff, however, was still determined, and he asked me to keep him overnight after Ruben went to work. Well, that was the deciding moment—I said "yes" and the puppy's been with us ever since.

Not that naming him was an easy decision, either. For nearly two weeks I searched through baby-naming books, mythology books—you name it. I simply felt no *simple* name would suffice for our new family member. As a young boy, we always had pets with regal names. My brother named our canary Ovis (Latin for "bird"), and our terrier Duncan after Shakespeare's work. (I broke the tradition when I named one of our dogs Mandy after the Barry Manilow song, but that's another story...)

Anyway, after our two-week search, eliminating contenders like Fabian, Astro and Cosmo, we turned to one of our favorite movies, *The Way We Were*. Fair-haired, all-American Hubbell Gardner, the character played by Robert Redford, seemed a perfect match for our fair-haired, all-American puppy. So, although people constantly ask me if we named him after the telescope, those in the know understand his true namesake. Maybe someday we'll get a little Katie to complete the family.

—Phil McKenna

Liza Reisenbach and LOUIE, VIOLET & LUCY

I love all my pets, and there is a unique story behind each of their names.

Louie, my white and shaggy Lhasa mix, came to me as a stray and was named after my ex-neighbor's dead grandfather, Grandpa Louie. Violet, a black mutt who weighs thirteen pounds, is kind of a "schnoodle." She was abandoned and abused, so she's aggressive, but timid—sort of a cross between a frail flower and a violent biting pooch who looks like a monkey. Lucy, my orange, long-haired cat, is named after the most famous Lucy of all, mainly so I could come home and say "Lucy, you have some 'splaining to do!" in a bad Cuban accent and not worry what the neighbors would think. Rosie, Lucy's sister, is also an orange, long-haired tabby, and I named her Rosie because I thought "Ethel" might be getting a little too obsessive. The newest addition to my family is Simba, a gorgeous grey tabby cat named after *The Lion King*. Just like him, my Simba is brave, daring and curious—all of which get him into some rather troublesome situations! In fact, he must be in one now—I haven't seen him in days, and I'm getting a little worried.

—Liza Reisenbach

Adam Peck and FRED

*T*he first Border Terrier I ever met lived in Westport, Connecticut. When the Ricardos moved to that very town on *I Love Lucy,* Little Ricky got a Border himself—coincidence? Hardly. I think there's clearly something much larger at work here. Ricky named his puppy Fred after lovable but curmudgeony Uncle Fred Mertz. Landlord, friend and former vaudevillian, he endures in our hearts as a proud, loyal and modest man from a bygone era. So I named my Border Terrier "Fred" too. What better tribute to one of television's greatest performers and most endearing characters?

—Adam Peck

Heather Langenkamp, Dave, Isabelle & Atticus and CHLOE, BUTTER WINDSOCK & MICKI

We found Chloe at a pet store. She was a neglected puppy who had been rescued from certain death, so we immediately decided to bring her home with us. Part Rottweiler, part Pit Bull, it took us only a few days to realize that her rather scary looks masked an underlying sweetness in her soul. So, as a play on her looks, we decided to give her a name that was both adorable and sweet. We chose Chloe.

It was October when our friend gave us a black cat named Elwood. We loved the cat, but we decided to let our son, Atticus, rename him. On Halloween, Atticus

saw a windsock hanging over the neighbors' doorway. Their dog, Sutter, was sitting beneath the windsock, and Atticus began saying "Sutter Butter Sutter Butter" like kids do. After a moment, Atticus looked up, beaming, and announced he wanted to name the cat "Butter Windsock."

Butter Windsock is the father of Mickeleideon—a more recent addition to our family—who is a black and white mix. Mickeleideon (Micki for short) was the name of Atticus's imaginary friend who visited our home for a good year and a half. When he stopped coming around, Atticus decided to honor him by naming our young kitten after him.

Most of our pets have come in pairs. We had Pride and Joy but they ran away. When we got our fish we decided to name them after our favorite food—Chips and Salsa. Sadly, Chips is no longer with us, but there's still plenty of Salsa.

—Heather Langenkamp

Susan Kite and RALPHIE ROTTEN

As a puppy with lots of brothers and sisters, I was always scared about finding a home. What if no one wanted me? Well, the first time I met my "mom" she didn't know she was going to be my mom. She was visiting the kennel with her dog, Alex, who was in for shots, so I thought I'd wander into the room, look cute (which, of course, I knew I was) and maybe I'd find myself a home.

I played it coy and acted like a real gentleman, hoping she'd notice me. I winked at her, showed off the whites of my eyes, and made quick friends with Alex. As it turned out, my brilliance paid off—she made arrangements to buy me! The only problem was, it would take about seven weeks before she could pick me up. So I waited patiently, dreaming of "Mom," counting down until The Big Day.

Finally it arrived, and boy, was I excited! *So* excited that on the way home, I piddled in the car. Then when we walked in the house and I saw all these other people and my friend, Alex, I just lost it. Within seconds, I became the worst little devil dog you've ever seen. For awhile I thought she might even take me back to the breeder's, but instead she kept me and named me "Ralphie Rotten—Puppy from Hell." She had grown up next door to a boy named Ralph who had the same hair color as me and was so bad everyone called him "Ralphie Rotten." I'll admit, the first couple of days I *tried* to be a good boy so she'd change my name, but I knew it was a losing battle. It's just not my nature to be good. So the name stuck, and I've been a little devil ever since.

—Ralphie Rotten
(as dictated to Susan Kite)

29

Lance Klein and LUCKY

A rock-n-roll megastar, whom I'll leave nameless, found my dog roaming in the hills of Ireland. He brought him back to the United States, but due to his heavy touring schedule, he couldn't take responsibility for the dog and decided to find him a good home. Since I was living in his guest house at the time, I just assumed the responsibility. When I moved out, I took him with me and he's still with me today. The rock star originally named him "Thoach" but I named him "Lucky" because he came from Ireland and had the luck of the Irish.

—Lance Klein

Teri Hatcher and BUKI & BONNIE

I was vacationing in Big Bear about ten years ago, and one of the houses down the street from the place I was renting had a sign in the window advertising Shar-Pei puppies. I guess I'd always thought Shar-Peis were cute, so I walked by the house to look at them. There in the window were these ten little puppies sitting on the edge of a couch, their scrunched-up faces all staring out at me. I was sold!

They were all so adorable, it was hard to pick one over the others, but eventually I chose "Kabuki" (named by the breeder, which I've never understood since Shar-Peis are Chinese). We shortened his name to just Buki.

I found my other dog, Bonnie, at the pound. She was a little puppy, and like all the other animals there, she looked like she needed a home. I love Bonnie Raitt, so I named the puppy in honor of her.

My three cats all have unusual names: Coltrane, a human-spirited, sexy black cat named in honor of John Coltrane's sexy music; Cienega, whom I found in the middle of La Cienega Boulevard in Los Angeles (thank God I got her off that busy street alive); and Tiberius, who has that emperor's regal character.

I also have a Cockatiel named Billy and a tortoise named Howard—only he fell in love with my neighbor's tortoise and they now share a love nest in a hole somewhere between our two backyards.

—Teri Hatcher

Steve Lukanic and GOGO

I'm not sure what exactly compelled me to get a cat. I was single, unattached, free to go where and when I pleased—no commitments, no real responsibilities. Oh yeah, now I remember. My life was a vacant *shell*—empty, lonely, void of any real purpose. I figured I had three options: get a relationship, get therapy, or get a pet.

I decided on a cat.

At first, I was a little nervous. I'd always grown up with dogs, and I'd *never* had a pet of my own. Should I start off with some fish? Maybe a bird or some type of lizard? Should I just get another philadendron and call it a day? Then a friend of mine told me that her friend's secretary's cat (swear to God) had just had kittens and they needed homes. Was I interested? Well, call me psychic, but I knew right then the tide was turning—my life, as I knew it, was about to change.

Sure enough, that night I drove to the secretary's house (in some remote part of town—I didn't know where the hell I was), and less than two hours later I was the proud father of this tiny little grey-striped *thing*. She was the runt of the litter, and as the secretary made up my "starter kit" (litter, kitty chow and a flea comb), this new kitten and I started bonding. All the way home, she curled up in my lap, obviously scared and a bit overwhelmed (especially when I started singing along to the radio). But once we got home, she immediately started to settle into her new surroundings, and after a few days, we were the best of pals.

I wasn't sure what to name her—I tried "Woobie," but I already knew someone with that name (it's a long story) and nothing else really *original* came to mind.

Then I remembered that since my little nephew could never say the word "uncle," he called me "gogo." Looking at my kitten, with her gray stripes and white "gogo boots," always on the "go" around the apartment, it seemed to fit. From that moment on, she was GoGo.

It's been over a year now since we met, and she really hasn't changed much. She's still small (I think it's the "runt" thing) and she still curls up in my lap and looks at me like I'm crazy every time I talk to her in my GoGo voice. She keeps me company while I work. She gets depressed every time I go out of town, and she's always waiting patiently in the window whenever I come home. Life without GoGo? I can't even imagine it.

Now maybe I should try a relationship?

—Steve Lukanic

Barb Treutelaar and Her Menagerie

I've loved animals for as far back as I can remember. My philosophy of my love for my pets has always been "they know everything about me and love me anyway!"

I started collecting strays when I was six years old and found Ricky, a black-and-white kitten I named after my crush at the time—Ricky Nelson. I've lost track of how many animals have passed through my doors over the years, and the cast seems to change daily. But right now my menagerie consists of the following:

My dogs, Jessica Lange (named because she has beautiful golden hair) and Spike (named because of his demeanor, or lack thereof). There's also Ashley (a.k.a.

"Killer") who doesn't live with me but occasionally drops by to visit (usually killing at least one rodent and *trying* to kill at least one chicken).

My cats—Greta Garbo, Sammy Davis, Jr., Grace Kelly, K.C. Sunshine Cat, Tom & Jerry, Woody (all white, named for Woody Harrelson in *White Cats Can't Jump*) and Spunky, who was given to me with that name.

My horses, Amber and Faby (mother and daughter). Faby is a nickname for "Your Fabulous Face," a song I was singing in a musical review at the time she was born. (I was there at her birth and she's always thought either I was a horse or she was a person.)

My rooster, Rudy Valentino, named for the way he "services" the hens; three black-and-white hens called The Pointer Sisters and one Rhode Island Red named Elizabeth Taylor (she's the most beautiful chicken in the world).

And my Harlequin macaw, simply named Harley, who loves to eat peanuts and sing songs from *Gypsy*.

I'd eventually like to add a pig to the collection—maybe even a monkey…as soon as I finish building the ark.

—Barb Treutelaar

J. Christopher Stucki and ZIPPY

My name's Zippy, and I live with Chris (or as I fondly refer to him, Food Source #1). We've been together almost eight years now, and he always tells me, "You dropped yourself in a bucket of butter the day I took you home." I, of course, zip away, pretending I don't need him. But between you and me, I thank my lucky nine lives for the day I first laid eyes on him.

My story begins nine years ago in Kalamazoo, Michigan. Snow blanketed the ground and the wind chill was below zero and falling. Despite my fur coat, I was freezing my butt off. I was hunkered down behind a snow bank, trying to stay out of the wind, when the headlights of a truck suddenly blinded me. Before I could turn and run, I was snatched up, tossed into the truck and taken down the road to a farmhouse. The lady farmer thought it best I stay with her and named me "Tippy" for the tip on my tail. (Not the most *original* name, but who was I to complain?)

I spent the rest of that winter and early spring on the farm—and it was wonderful! I'd spend my days darting through the chicken coop, racing through the horse stables, jumping over fences, running through the barn, bolting up trees and tearing through the garden. It was a country cat's life and I loved every minute of it! That is, until the other cats began to complain to the farmer. Apparently they didn't approve of my fast-paced lifestyle and thought it best I move on to greener pastures. So, just as I packed up my catnip, ready to hit the road, the lady farmer entered the barn with a tall shadowy figure: "Here's Tippy." And with that I was snatched up again and tossed into the arms of Chris.

I moved to Chicago with Chris where I spent the next few years racing down flights of stairs, meowing at the taxis on the street, pushing pens off the desk, jumping into bags, watching the Cubs and zipping through the apartment. It was a city cat's life and I loved every minute of it! But because of my wild antics and crazy ways, Chris started to call me by a more appropriate name—Zippy!

Now we live in California, and I'm still living up to my new name. I zip around his wife, Catherine (Food Source #2), zip over my baby brother, Jake (*Future* Food Source #3), zip through the house, zip out the door, zip back in the door, zip down the stairs, zip across the bed, zip from the floor to the couch to Chris' lap— and on and on through the rest of my nine lives.

—Zippy
(as dicatated to Food Source #1)

Kerry Tsakonas and NIKKI & CASSIE

Our ten-year-old yellow Lab's name is Cassie, but we affectionately call her "Casper The Friendly Pooch." She was actually named after a soap opera character (I'm embarassed to say!). It wasn't that I had a particular bond with the character—I just liked the sound of the name. Cass is an amazing companion who thinks she's human.

The suggestion of getting some company for Cassie in the form of a four-legged friend was not well received by my husband, John. So imagine my surprise on December 24, 1994, when he casually walked in the front door, gently holding a befuddled eight-week-old yellow Lab puppy. After much discussion, we opted to call her Saint Nikki, since she came to live with us on Christmas Eve. She is by far the best surprise and Christmas gift I've ever had! She's been a wonderful and energetic addition to our family, and fortunately Cassie agrees.

—Kerry Tsakonas

Marcy Bolotin & Lawrence Paull and MAX & SADIE

Sadie, our Bearded Collie, and Max, our English Springer Spaniel, were Larry's and my Valentine's Day presents to one another. We adopted them as adult dogs after they'd been given up (or in Max's case, abandoned) by previous owners.

Sadie was a former show dog (her full name is Mercedes Fortune) from Omaha, Nebraska. We flew her to Los Angeles, sight unseen, and fell in love with her immediately. Nicknamed Sadie by her former owners, we've added one more affectionate name—Pussy or The Puss, because she has the sweetest face.

Max was adopted from a spaniel rescue out in the Valley. He had been found wandering the streets and luckily was brought to the animal shelter. Larry didn't like his original name, Marcus, and selected Max because of the similiarity of the sound. He's the biggest nudge and we fondly refer to him as "adore-a-dog!"

—Marcy Bolotin

Matthew Margolis and ULLI & TILLIE

I knew I wanted German Shepherds because they are the most obedient, intelligent dogs. Ulli, my male Shepherd, came from Germany and was already named. Tillie, my female Shepherd, was named after my wife's Aunt Tillie, who was very classy and well dressed. My Tillie is a tough little girl, mischievous as hell, but the name still suits her. The dogs love each other. They're the best of friends and the ultimate partners.

—Matthew Margolis

Tyler & Parker Cary and ROY & JET

I did chores to earn money to buy my iguana. My little brother got his for his birthday. The man at the pet store said the vet will tell us if they're boys or girls when they are two years old. For now, we named the big one Roy the Iguana Boy and the little one Jet the Iguana Pet. Iguanas are really cool because they look like dinosaurs and shed their skin! We sit with them in the bathtub so they won't be afraid of us and run away.

—Tyler Cary

Lynne White and HOWIE

Howie and I met in the spring of 1989. He was in his fifteenth year, I was in my...well, let's just say *not* my fifteenth year. His owners had left him long ago, and he was about to lose his latest caretaker when I took over his lease. I've been told he spent his earlier years as a Grand Prix Jumper named Spectator and that he was nicknamed Howie after Howard Cosell—the ultimate sports spectator.

Howie is now twenty-one, although more often than not he displays the heart and hijinks of a two-year-old. He's been a wonderful addition to our family, and we look forward to many more years of play together.

—Lynne White

Ricky Frazier and NORTON

My first bird, Bomber, died and after his funeral I kept looking for another one. Nine months later, I walked into a pet store and found Norton. He's such a great little guy, and we're the best of friends. He loves to play golf with me, ride around on miniature remote-controlled cars, and we even sing a duet version of "That's Amore!" (better than Dean Martin).

I named him after Art Carney's character, Ed Norton, in *The Honeymooners*, my favorite TV show. Norton's too.

—Ricky Frazier

Kari & Dick Clark and MAYBELLINE, MOLLY, BERNARDO & LUCILLE

*F*irst we had Mort, an old black Lab that Dick won at an auction. We knew a dog at the beach named Mort, who was really the king of the beach, so we named our dog Mort, too! Then we got him a girlfriend, and since we knew he was part Weimaraner, we got a purebred Weimaraner and named her Molly, as in Jerry Lee Lewis' "Good Golly Miss Molly." Eventually Mort and Molly had puppies, and we kept one and named her Maybelline in honor of Chuck Berry.

Our Dalmation, Lucille, was a gift from Gloria Estefan. Her two dogs, Lucy and Ricky, had puppies, so she gave us one and we named her Lucille after her mom.

We found our other dog, Bernardo, on a street in San Bernardino, and named him accordingly! We think he's part Dachsund, part Lab, and though we thought he was a puppy when we found him, he was already two years old. To this day, no one ever calls him Bernie or Bern—always Bernardo!

—Kari & Dick Clark

Rudy Wilson and RACINE

Once upon a time, Mommy and Daddy went to buy a puppy. All the other puppies in the litter were leaping at the fence, begging to be chosen. Except one. She lingered in the background, watching them, and they liked that attitude. They liked it so much they decided to keep her and give her a name to match. A sassy, take-no-prisoners kind of name. A name like Racine.

As a puppy, Racine had a fuzzy face. She had a tiny little tail and she went pee pee in a flowerpot. She ate an angel off the Christmas tree. She got lost, and Mommy and Daddy looked all over for her (she was in the front of the house, hiding). Now she's bigger, and she's got a big tail and she makes a big noise when Daddy comes home. Racine is my best friend.

And she's still got attitude.

—Rudy Wilson

Captain Haggerty and MR. CAT

I've had animal buddies over the years with some of the simplest, silliest names you could imagine. There's my parrot, Polly (yes, she usually does want a cracker); my ball python, Bull, named because he's as strong as one; my best buddy of all, Mr. Cat (he looks just like one); and an American Cocker Spaniel named Spot (because he has none).

I also had a German Shepherd, who never should have been called Fido so I changed the spelling to Phideaux; a Pit Bull Terrier named Miss Crunch because that's the noise she made chewing bones; Mr. Dog, the first animal I had with a "mister" or "miss" title—I was commanding the 25th Infantry Scout Dog Platoon at the time. And last but not least, there was an English Bull Terrier—Ch. Loveland's Windy McLain. I got him when the previous owner couldn't control him, and I made a champion out of him. His name was appropriate because he always passed gas. Or at least I blamed him!

—Captain Haggerty

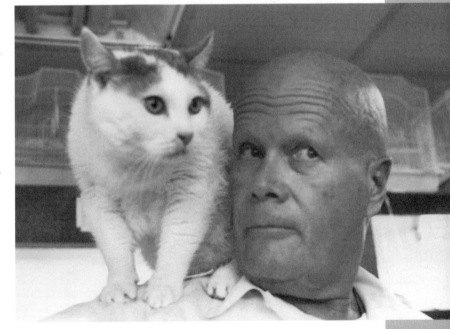

45

Stephanie Zimbalist and DIPPY

My mother was driving on an access road near the freeway in Burbank around Christmas 1987, and she saw this little white dirty thing scurrying like a bullet. Being the inveterate animal saver she is (and quite well known in that arena), my ma always has dog biscuits in the back of her car, so she began throwing some toward the dog. She finally followed the puppy into someone's yard, at which point the puppy stopped running, exhausted by the chase. She gradually lured the little mutt into her hands and took her home to the huge menagerie in my parents' house—she joined the "kitchen" dogs, as we call them, because every time you walk in the kitchen they leap all over you for attention!

I was doing a play in New York in 1991 and found myself stopping *every* dog I'd see on the street and talking to it. My dog, Clarence, had died about twelve years before, and I knew it was time for another. When I told my mother I wanted

a dog, she said, "Take Dippy." I wasn't even sure which one of the pack "Dippy" was—oh yeah, the circus dog who jumps. Well, I took her home, and right away this new personality emerged; she had been begging for attention for years, lost in the pile of other dogs. Now she was a one-person dog with *no* competition—it was as if she died and went to heaven!

Dip's my pal, my child—she softens my heart and guards her fort. It's actually *her* house, and she lets me stay there, too. She travels wherever I go (she's been on thirty-seven airplanes, and I keep an itinerary of every place she visits), and whenever I'm on the set or in the theater, she's always in my dressing room. She's a "glue" that brings people together, which is so great at work. Arms unfold, smiles appear, people immediately cluck over her and open their hearts. That's the best part about dogs—they're truly ambassadors of goodwill.

—Stephanie Zimbalist

Dan Ferris and EDDIE

One night I was walking over to visit a friend, minding my own business, and I saw this little black-and-white dog running around in a yard. I stopped the lady I assumed was the owner and asked her several questions about the dog—"Is that a Jack Russell terrier?" She said yes. She also said she was "disgusted" with the dog and wanted to give him away. Within an hour she gave him to me. Of course, I had to think of a name fast, and he was running around fast in the yard, so the name of a character in a Barbra Streisand movie I liked popped into mind: "Fast Eddie"…Eddie for short.

—Dan Ferris

Linda Gray and GIORGIO

I grew up with dogs, and I've never had a span of time without one. When we first moved to our ranch, I had a German Shepherd named Gunnar and a sheep dog named Michael. They died in the same year and I was devastated. It broke my heart. So for Christmas, my daughter and my son presented me with this wonderful little German Shepherd puppy, with the best personality and energy that never stopped! He was like a kid with too much candy, zooming around the house, and his favorite trick soon became chewing on a pair of shoes I had just bought on a trip to Milan. (I wasn't too crazy about it, but I figured it was just a bad phase.)

I hadn't named him yet, but seeing him chew on those shoes, I thought back to my trip to Italy, where I had had the pleasure of meeting Mr. Giorgio Armani. He was such a a wonderful man, full of style and class, and so elegant and creative. I wanted to translate those same traits to my dog! I figured he already knew good quality fashion when it came to the shoes he liked to chew, and I was certain he showed tremendous promise in the other areas as well.

So even though he was this wild, crazy *German* Shepherd, I decided to make him Italian and name him Giorgio! He no longer chews expensive shoes, but he's still the most stylish, classy, elegant dog I know.

—Linda Gray

49

Billy Koch & Kathy Kaehler and CLYDE, MOOSE & BEAR

We have three, count 'em *three*, black Labrador Retrievers…

Clyde

He's named after Clyde "the Glyde" Drexler of the Portland Trailblazers and always wears a red collar (the Blazers' colors are black and red). He's sleek, fast and strong and a tremendous athlete.

Bear

The first time we saw him he actually looked like a tiny little bear cub, only he was fat—so fat, his stomach touched the ground when he walked. Now we affectionately call him Pooh, or Pooh Bear, referring to the classic tale of Winnie.

Moose

When the Dallas Cowboys won the Super Bowl in 93, one of the heroes was their fullback, Darryl "Moose" Johnston. Whenever he touched the ball, the entire stadium chanted "MOOOOOOOOOSE!" We fell in love with the name (and the "animal" motif) and decided to name our puppy "The Moose." Best way to describe him? He's a tank.

—Billy Koch & Kathy Kaehler

Maria Bell and TRACY & HEPBURN

I got Tracy right after my first Maltese, Garbo, died. I knew no one could replace Garbo, so I decided that having two dogs—a dynamic duo—would make for a different experience and fill the enormous gap in my life. That's when I got Hepburn. I had always been a movie buff and always loved the chemistry between Spencer Tracy and Katherine Hepburn, and amazingly my new dogs' personalities fit their movie star counterparts perfectly! Tracy is a lovable lug, easygoing and down-to-earth, and Hepburn is much more wily, canny, and just a little high strung. They have an incredible give-and-take relationship. Hepburn is a pound smaller and always fights harder to get her way, but Tracy keeps her in line. They're so adorable and so well loved, and since they split their time between our house and my grandparents, they are definitely in demand. Of course, they'll never have the fame and fortune the real Tracy and Hepburn enjoyed...but they'll always have top billing with us.

—Maria Bell

Barb & Tom Hoke and STELLA & GUSSIE

Our cats have several names; if you saw the play *Cats*, you know what I'm talking about. Gus (a.k.a. Gussie Girl, Gussafers, Gussafer-Jones) was born at the end of October 1986. A producer on the television show I was working on knew I was in the market for a kitty, and her cat had just given birth. She brought in this batch of little black-and-white furballs…one look at Gussie and I knew she was for me! I'm not really sure why I named her Gus. I think this friend of Tom's used to call him that, so I figured why not call the cat that, too?

Stella (a.k.a. My Big Girl, Stellie-Bellie) came via a friend of ours who loved animals and had nine cats at his house. Stella had appeared at his doorstep one day with a name tag but no place to call home. He asked if I was interested in getting a playmate for Gus since she was home alone so much. All I had to do was take one look at this gorgeous, grey, big, fat cat with green eyes, and I fell in love again. I took her home that night and she and Gus became best friends (eventually). As for her name, how could I change it? Stella it was and Stella it stayed.

Now when I come home at night, they go right to their bowls and yell at me until I feed them. When Tom gets home they fall at his feet and rub up against him (of course, so do I). What more can we say? We love them—we *think* they love us. And we can't imagine our lives without them!

—Barb Hoke

Elizabeth Kee and MISS LUCY DAISY GIRL & MR. DESI LUCKY GUY

Miss Lucy Daisy Girl is our little princess. She was a lost dog, and when we first got her, we didn't know she was a purebred miniature Schnauzer. But after she was cleaned up and fed and loved, she revealed her true breed. At first she was just Daisy…

Then along came Mr. Desi Lucky Guy, a macho black miniature Schnauzer with a pedigree a mile long. We got him from a pet shop—he was going on six months, and they were looking to get rid of him because he was no longer a puppy.

We didn't want anything bad to happen to such a sweet and precocious dog, so we took him home and called him "Mr. Lucky Guy" (since we saved him).

Right away Daisy and Mr. Lucky Guy loved each other. So, since our daughter, Elizabeth, loves the old *I Love Lucy* series, we decided to name Daisy "Miss *Lucy* Daisy Girl" to match "Mr. *Desi* Lucky Guy." We believe they are, indeed, a "lucky guy" and "lucky girl" to be found just in the nick of time and welcomed into a good, loving home.

—Sydney Ann, Gordon & Elizabeth Kee

Tisha Campbell & Duane Martin and ASHLEY, BASIL & ONYX

Our oldest dog is Ashley and there's no particular reason why she got that name—Duane just looked in her face and she looked like an Ashley! As for Basil—one of Duane's favorite Italian dishes has basil in it, so since Basil was part of the ingredients of our family, the name seemed right. Onyx and Sojah (Sojah's not in the picture with us) got their names because Duane gave them to me, and I call him my "black soldier."

—Tisha Campbell & Duane Martin

Nance Mitchell and FLOWER

I have a niece, Candi, who has a three-year-old daughter, Caitlin. For Christmas one year, they gave me this little fawn-colored Pekingese, but we weren't sure what to name her. So we sat Caitlin down and asked her if she had any ideas. She had just watched the Disney movie, *Bambi,* and loved the skunk, Flower. That was it!

Since then, *my* Flower has been in her own movie (*Big Bucks for Buddha*—she plays "Fifi"). She's been photographed for many different exhibitions, and won several ribbons. I'm so proud of her, and I look forward to many more years together!

—Nance Mitchell

Paul Kaplan and MUSSOLINI

I have had bad luck with fish. I clean the tank, I treat the water, I rent them movies (*Jaws* is a favorite), and yet they always die. It's a sad moment when you arrive home from work to find your little friend floating lifeless at the top of his aquarium.

It's painful to watch him circling around the toilet bowl before finally entering his portal to fishy heaven. This traumatic experience is made worse by the fact that the fish is always named after a girlfriend, favorite movie star, or sports hero. You're not just flushing a fish, you're flushing "Eel Pacino."

That's why I named my current fish Mussolini. I figured if I came home to find him dead I could say, "Damn fish was a facist anyway!" Of course Mussolini (the fish) has lived for two years—which is exactly one year and eleven months longer than any other fish I have ever owned. The worst part is, I don't feel comfortable buying any other fish to keep Mussolini company. I just don't feel right exposing them to his dangerous politics.

—Paul Kaplan

Kimberly Conrad Hefner and Her World of Beautiful Animals at the Playboy Mansion

One of the truly special highlights of putting this book together was my visit with Kimberly Conrad Hefner at the Playboy Mansion. Kimberly and her family have such an incredible array of exotic creatures that an entire book could probably be devoted solely to them!

I hardly knew what to expect upon visiting this world-famous mansion, but I felt very much at home as soon as I entered the grounds. Even though it was midweek and our staff was invading her home, Kimberly was the most gracious hostess. She was bright, cheerful and above everything else, she demonstrated a knowledge and love for her pets that was nothing short of amazing.

The mansion and its grounds are home to over 100 animals and fish, including at least seven dogs, scores of exotic birds (peacocks, flamingos, African Crown Cranes, incredible parrots, pigeons, doves, ducks), rabbits, turtles, lizards, horny toads, snakes, an iguana, saltwater fish, tropical fish, and the wildest member of them all—a woolly monkey! Many of the animals are endangered and were either rescued or donated to this loving environment (which, by the way, has a full-time staff of vets and attendants).

Wherever we walked, one or more of these creatures would follow along. Flamingos wandered around in an orderly pack, ducks quacked away, occasionally taking a break to dip in the pool, and dogs somehow contained themselves from racing around. We heard squawks and animal sounds of all imaginable types. It was as though we were on a private safari in the middle of the city!

But even more extraordinary—and perhaps the thing that impressed us the most—was that Kimberly seems to have a special bond with each and *every* animal. She nurtures them, spends time with them, and makes sure they are all loved. And in a virtual zoo of every type of animal imaginable, she knows every one of their names!

—*Wendy Nan Rees*

Evann Wilkerson and DODGER

I was visiting my grandparents and we went to the pet store one day and saw some baby rats. I asked the lady at the store where the rats were going, and she told me they were going to a lab. So I begged my dad to *please* let me get one of the rats—and that's how I got Dodger. (I picked him because he was jumping all over my hand.) Then, when I got home, he accidentally got out of his cage, and we were frantic! Our cats were sniffing around…it was horrible. I finally found him, but he escaped from the cage again a couple months later. Sometimes he can be a nightmare…sometimes he can be really cool. We have another rat, Goliath, and he loves Dodger—they're just really fun together. Some people think it's really unusual for me to have rats, but I love them a lot!

—Evann Wilkerson

Lauralee Bell and BERNIE & HARLEY

Harley is a Poodle, but we wanted to give her a non-Poodle sounding name. On her first day with us we were having a big party and asked the guests to help us choose a name. People wrote down everything from "Fluffy" and "Muffy" to "Spike" and "Killer"—none of which seemed appropriate. A few days later I came up with Harley, and after a few jokes about a leather-clad Poodle straddling a motorcycle in a Hell's Angels run, everybody loved it. As for Bernie, our Saint Bernard, we got her several years ago as a puppy, along with her brother. They looked so much alike, we named them Bernie (short for Bernice) and Barney. (Sadly, Barney now watches over us from Doggie Heaven.)

—Lauralee Bell

Dylan McDonald and DOOGIE

I have a pet named Doogie.

He is called Doogie because he is black and white.

I take good care of Doogie because he's my puppy.

The End.

—Dylan McDonald

Noah Wyle and CHAR & MICK

Mick is the son of my father's cat—he was the cutest one of the litter, and I have no idea why I named him Mick. I mean, I *know* why I named him Mick, it's just embarrassing to say—at the time I was with my ex-girlfriend, Kim, and if you switch her name around you get Mik. (I thought it was a cute romantic thing to do.) But now I've added a "c" to his name, so you can forget the whole story.

My dog, Charlotte, was a gift from my downstairs neighbor, Marty, who rescued her from certain destruction from this hillbilly couple who had a pack of wild dogs that were all beaten and malnourished. She was the baby of the litter, and he just fell in love with her and brought her home to me. I named her Charlotte—well, actually my same ex-girlfriend, Kim, named her Charlotte because she was obsessed with the book *Charlotte's Web*. But now I just call her Char, so you can forget the whole story.

—Noah Wyle

Jane Oppenheimer & Matt Sheehan and FLORA

Our black Labrador Retriever is named Flora, but when she was born we had asked the man looking after her to call her Edith. It was the least petlike name we could come up with, and somehow we thought it would be humorous to have a dog with such a ridiculously human name. At three months, the vet deemed Edith old enough to get in a crate and fly across the country from Boston to meet us (finally) in Los Angeles. I was so excited about her arrival, I phoned my equally dog-obsessed father to tell him about the puppy en route. When he learned she was to be known as Edith, he was outraged, thinking it was much too serious and mature for the unstoppable, goofy personality of a Lab. He mentioned that he had

been to a dinner party the night before and it struck him that the name of his hostess was the appropriate name for our new best friend…Flora! It perfectly suited our thoughts of who our dog was to be, and it is truly who she has become.

—Jane Oppenheimer

Heather Tom and WESLEY

I decided I wanted a dog, and after my last experience with a Beagle (which was horrible!), I decided to get a Poodle. I had grown up with Poodles, so I knew what to expect. So, I went to my breeder and picked up "Wesley," the runt of the litter, and kind of funny looking. He had one ear that stood straight out and legs that were abnormally long! Anyway, my roommates and I tossed around a few names—Chaplin, Sack, Winston—but none of them fit. I've always been a fan of nice, normal, everyday names... nothing fancy. Wesley was such a small dog, and he was and still is such a momma's boy (that's me) that a name like "Wesley" just fit. It's kind of wimpy, but cute at the same time.

—Heather Tom

Peter & Robin Saisselin and
OTIS & VERONICA

I inherited Veronica when I took my first apartment in L.A. Her owner left her behind ("Sorry!" she said) when she packed her bags for New York. I named her Veronica after the actress, Veronica Lake. Like her, my cat was petite, purring and seductive, and she got what she wanted. She had a free ticket with me and she rode it all the way. She was an indoor/outdoor cat and I was at her beck and call (which usually came at 6 am). I made the mistake of introducing her to canned food. She's never been off the stuff since. A starlet in the truest sense.

When I got married, my wife, Robin, needed a cat of her own. Her cat of twenty-one years, Groucho-Maria, had recently passed away. She went to the pet adoption agency and found a little black-and-white kitten behind the caged doors. Voted "most unadoptable," he wasn't meowing like the other cats vying for her attention. Rather, he was turned away facing the back of the cage—lonely and dejected. (He could have been Rudolph after the reindeer tryouts.) The minute she picked him up he started purring. He was hers. He was, however, the product of that nasty animal habit called inbreeding. He has a small head, crossed eyes, a big belly, and as my wife likes to say, a "big pink nose." Plain and simple, he's mentally challenged. We named him Otis, and I like to think of him as an "idiot savant" since he gets everything he asks for even though he's mute. The poor guy can't even meow—he only squeaks—nor can he jump (instead, he pulls

himself up the arm of the couch). But he's a great cat, and we love him. Of course, the problem was getting Veronica to love him . . .

Otis disappeared two weeks after we got him. We looked high and low and deduced he must have fallen off our second-floor balcony. After two lonely weeks, we found him one night. Though Robin and I can't prove it—evidence had been compromised, paw prints smudged, hair fibers licked away—we suspect Veronica may have pushed him over the edge or encouraged him to jump. She's very protective of me and I think jealousy got the best of her.

Since then, the two seem to get along. He wants to play, she doesn't. He wants to meow, she never stops. She's accepted Otis and he—well, I don't even know if he realizes she's another cat. He's happy to be loved and we're happy to have them both.

—Peter Saisselin

Courtney Thorne-Smith
and GEORGE & ED

I rescued my dogs from the Basenji Rescue, and I wanted to name them big, tough, macho names so they'd defend me. I picked George and Ed—like bowling buddies. And then they promptly fell in love with each other, so it was all for naught!

—Courtney Thorne-Smith

Josh Levinson and BRANDY

A couple of years ago I spent my summer exploring the back roads of Italy on a motorcycle. In a small town outside of Florence I met Brandy. She was a British art student studying abroad, and we immediately fell in love. For the next glorious weeks we cruised the Italian countryside together on my motorcycle. When I got back to the States I was enveloped with loneliness. To keep me company I bought a fish and, of course, I named it Brandy…

Wow, it would be so cool if even a shred of that story were true. What *really* happened was someone gave me a fish in a brandy snifter for my birthday. I figured brandy snifter, what the hell, might as well name the little guy Brandy.

Still, I would like to go to Italy some day.

—Josh Levinson

Molly Shaw & Michael Runnels and ELVIS, DUKE & HOYA

Since I'm a big fan of college basketball, I named our cat, Duke, after the Duke Blue Devils (he has big blue eyes) and our other cat, Hoya, after the Georgetown Hoyas. Sometimes they drive us absolutely *crazy*, but overall, I'd say we're having a pretty good season.

Mike chose the name Elvis for our dog because he's a huge fan of Elvis Costello (even though everyone always thinks it was in honor of that other guy).

—Molly Shaw

Lori Roberts and CLOUD

Several years ago my sister rescued a kitten from an uncaring man who didn't want kittens running wild on his ranch. He was going to "take care of them," he told her, so she quickly rescued one from the litter. As she held the kitten in the palm of her hand, she lifted her up toward the sky and the kitty blended perfectly with the billowy white clouds. So she became a "Cloud," too.

She's part Siamese (she has the crooked tail, the meow, the blue eyes, and very faint points on her face) but her beautiful white fur coat obviously suggests another breed.

Cloud lives with me now, and though she doesn't get outside much, I do occasionally catch her staring out the window, looking longingly up at the sky. Family and friends have given her multiple nicknames, including Little Miss, Brat, Priss, Kick-R-in-the-Butt and Miss Kitty—but I think she loves Cloud the best.

—Lori Roberts

Jack Murray and LUKE

There was a knock on the door. I opened it and saw nothing until this tiny bear cub puppy with a soft, fuzzy head walked in and sat down. He was a surprise from friends. He said his name was Luke…short for "Babaluca Maphuzhead" (my fuzz head).

—Jack Murray

Kristin Stuart and VLADIMIR

Vladimir was the first cat that came to me. He was this teeny little kitten with huge ears that made him look like a bat. I had just seen *Bram Stoker's Dracula* and I remembered the story of Vlad the Impaler. "Vlad" sealed the deal when I brought him home and he proved himself to be a great warrior against a roll of toilet paper, impaling it with his sharp, tiny claws.

Isabelle came next. I was looking for a suitable girlfriend for Vlad and my neighbor's cat happened to have kittens around that time. Her mother, Claire, had a French name so I thought I'd stick with that notion. It suits her perfectly, because she's very coquettish and feminine.

My cat Woody came to me already christened and full grown. He is Woody, hear him roar! He's my all-American cat and he loves to defend his territory.

My other cat, Sophie, had the original name Soul Food, named after the Manhattan Transfer song, "Soul Food to Go," which was playing on the tape deck when she walked in the room. She was extremely passionate and I later came to discover she was in heat. I brought her home with the blessings of her former owner who wasn't quite sure how to handle such a lusty gal. Soul Food quickly became abbreviated to Sophie (I felt ridiculous beckoning her to come in for her supper with "Here, Soul Food!"). She's my wild woman, my femme fatale, who still enjoys staying out late with the boys.

—Kristin Stuart

72

Joe Lando and ROSEBUD

I adopted Rosie (a.k.a. Rosebud) from a family with work dogs out on the ranch where we film *Dr. Quinn, Medicine Woman*. She was a "mistake"—a heat-of-the-moment type of thing between two of the work dogs. (Otherwise, I probably would have gone to the pound to get a dog.) Now she comes to work with me every-

day, come hell or high water, easily spending twelve hours or more with me. She's named Rosie because the family we adopted her from had the last name "Rose"—but she's also named Rosebud after the sleigh in the movie, *Citizen Kane*. Of everything Citizen Kane had, his sleigh was the most important thing. And Rosebud is my most treasured possession, too.

—Joe Lando

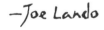

June

It was a Monday in June, 5:30 at night on death row at the animal shelter. The animals scheduled to be destroyed had two hours left to live. One of the doomed was a huge one-year-old German Shepherd/Doberman mix that nobody wanted. On assignment to find a cute puppy for a friend, instead I spotted her. Her giant ears stuck straight up like antennae to Mars, and she looked like a fruit bat sporting a big toothy smile. With the intelligent head of a Shepherd and the agile body of a Doberman, she was quite unique, even stunning, under the ten pounds of grime and protruding bones. But it was her eyes that haunted me all the while I walked up and down those barking rows upon rows of caged eager faces, all promising to love someone—anyone—if given a chance. Though I lived in an apartment and had no intention of getting a dog, I could not get her face out of my mind. Surely she could find a home…right? When I asked an employee, I learned she was to be destroyed that night.

Well, I've made a few bad decisions in my life, but one of the best and dearest things I've ever done I did that evening. I brought home a friend and named her June.

Margie Sunshine

Her registered name is Margie Sunshine—my big, beautiful, bay Quarter Horse mare. (The "Sunshine" is a namesake of the Palm Springs ranch where she was foaled). Alias Margie, Marge the Barge, and Large Marge (yes, her rump is of generous proportions), she is, truly, one of the sweetest horses I've ever known. Kind and gentle, she takes care of anyone on her back. I attribute such a considerate attitude to her propensity for daydreaming and enjoying the trail as much as her rider—a poetic way of saying she's extremely lazy (at times, a slug with bad corns lays a faster track). She's a wonderful companion who gives great peace and joy to those who straddle her back and head for the hills.

—Jana Howington

Joan, Ralph, Katherine & Elizabeth Singleton and JASPER, EMMY, OSCAR, PEEPERS & CINNAMON

Oscar and Emmy—how could there be Hollywood dogs without Hollywood names? They're brother and sister, now ten years old, and they each have such distinct personalities. Oscar is a Rottweiler in a Poodle's body. He's chased and killed more backyard gophers than we can count, attacked a rattlesnake (and was bitten), and chased a coyote, who then caught *him* and gave him six puncture wounds.

Emmy, on the other hand, is a perfect little lady—crossed paws and all. She loves to preen in the mirror and sit in your lap and be stroked.

Jasper, the king of the roost, is over twelve years old. A wild little guy from the beginning, he too, tangled with a rattlesnake and almost died. He has taught himself how to crawl on his belly like GI Joe, knock over small pieces of furniture and use them to crawl onto higher plateaus, and make everyone who meets him want to adopt him.

We also have two other members of the family: Peepers, the rat, and Cinnamon, a baby white-faced Cockatiel, who drives the dogs absolutely crazy.

Whoever thinks Poodles are pampered pets that sit around all day on satin pillows hasn't met the three of ours!

—Joan, Ralph, Katherine & Elizabeth Singleton

Anthony Edwards & Jeanine Lobel and EVE

At first I had a black-and-white cat named Adam, named after the police car in *Adam 12*. Then one day, these kids were selling magazine subscriptions and introduced me to this stray dog they had found—a Labrador and Pit Bull mix. They asked if I would try to find her owner. I said I would—so I hung fliers and ads all over the neighborhood, but no one ever claimed her. I had one of those half doors at the house, and after wandering around all those days, she finally jumped over the door, into my house, and made the choice that that's where she wanted to be. Since I had the cat named Adam, I named her Eve. And she became the First Lady.

—Anthony Edwards

Donna, Tracy & Hannah Nash and DAVE

Our first cat, Marley, was named after Bob Marley, whom we were big fans of at the time. Jimmy Cliff, another reggae singer, inspired the name of our second cat, Clifford. The name of our third cat was a little more involved. Basically, a friend came to pick up one of two stray kittens we were taking care of, and he told us his long-held desire to name a cat—any cat—Dave. Since his girlfriend already had a name for their new pet, we decided to keep the other stray and name *her* Dave. Of course, our daughter, Hannah, prefers to call them all just "keetees."

—Donna & Tracy Nash

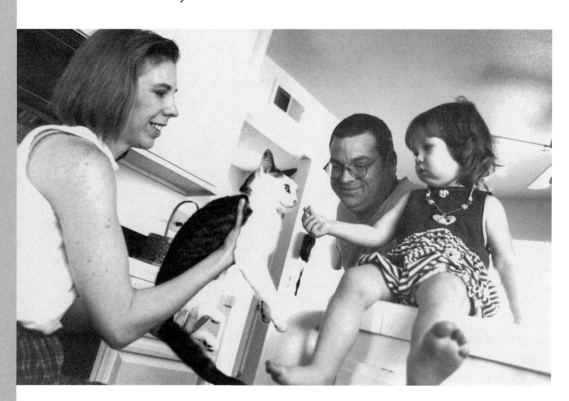

Merrill Markoe and LEWIS, WINKY, TEX & BO

My naming pattern has always been this: Try to pick pet names that had no cute-adorable-cuddly associations whatsoever. The names of my previous two dogs, Bob and Stan, fulfilled this requirement. This is also how I named my big dog Lewis. It seemed as inappropriate and un-petlike a name as I could come up with. Other names on this list, for any future pets I might name, would be Ed, Debbie, Ken, Linda, Carlos, Lyle, Roland, and Donna.

Which does not explain why I broke form and named my little dog Winky. The only explanation I have is that the day I picked him up strolling along Pacific Coast Highway without tags I didn't think I would keep him. I had three dogs and that seemed like a full dance card to me. I started calling him Winky because it's a word I use interchangeably with "goofball" and it's all I could think of when I would come home and see him spinning around and around in the corner, showing how glad he was to see me. At that point he hardly knew me. He couldn't have been *that* happy. But after three or four days of this, I started to be glad to see him, too. And by then, the name had already taken hold.

My other two dogs, Tex and Bo, came to me with names already in place. Tex was rescued from a homeless man who died. And Bo used to belong to my neighbors, but moved in with me once he got a look at what a higher standard of dog living I was offering—and what a bad grasp I had of the idea of pet control.

—Merrill Markoe

Ruth & Howard W. Koch, Sr. and OSCAR

I've always loved animals, especially dogs. I also loved making a film called *The Odd Couple* with Walter Matthau and Jack Lemmon. Walter Matthau's character's name in the picture was Oscar, and that's how our Labrador got his name.

Before Oscar, we had a German Shepherd named Wally—also named after Walter Matthau—and a French Poodle named Pierre after Pierre Cossette. I had walked off a plane with Pierre Cossette, who had just gotten the Poodle, so I took the new pup and named it after him.

After Pierre, we had a Dalmatian, Pebbles, named for his black spots which resembled little stones.

But perhaps one of my most cherished pets was Telly's Pop, a beautiful dark bay racehorse that I owned with Telly Savalas. The "Telly" is self-explanatory and so is the "Pop"—short for lollipop.

—Howard W. Koch, Sr.

Shelby Marlo and LOTTE & RUBY

Pearl was Lotte's predecessor, and she left a lot to live up to. Pearl was the kind of dog you get once in a lifetime if you're lucky. She and I were so connected that, in my overwrought teenage mind, I decided I could not live without her and would kill myself when she died. Needless to say, I reconsidered. But when she was old and failing, I decided I needed a puppy that resembled Pearl, a Collie mix, as much as possible. This led me on a long quest, which finally ended with my Smooth Collie, Lotte. She's named after Lotte Lena, a singer, actress and the wife of Kurt Weil, who composed *The Three Penny Opera*.

In trying to fill the void left by Pearl, I discovered my future with Lotte. I'm a lifelong animal lover, but it was when I immersed myself in training Lotte that I realized the gift I had could be a career. The rest is what I refer to as my Cinderella story. I began entering competition obedience trials and much to my surprise, Lotte won every time. She became the top-ranked obedience Collie in the United States, and the first Smooth Collie in history to have won that title. And to top it all, we even had the coveted ribbon presented to us by Lassie herself!

Enter Bad Dog Ruby. After years of building my career as an animal behavior specialist and trainer, I got to start all over again with Ruby. I was buying the "house that dogs built" and I decided I needed a guard dog. A trainer friend of mine had just finished up a movie about a genetically manipulated killer dog. He had used Tibetan Mastiffs, which look like long-haired Rottweilers with curly tails. Eight of these dogs guard the

Dalai Lama's summer house and I figured that was good enough for me. My friend gave me a puppy and I agonized over her name. I borrowed books on Tibet, but I decided Dharma was too "new age." And though I considered Dolly, in the end Ruby just felt right.

And so I moved into my new house, with my award-winning Collie, Lotte, and my great defender, Ruby. All is well at the homestead, except for one small adjustment: instead of Ruby guarding my house, I've ended up guarding my house from her. That's why her official registered name is Bad Dog Ruby.

—Shelby Marlo

Susan, Bill & Nick Moores and GABRIEL & JASMINE

We knew Gabriel was nothing less than an angel when his four pounds of silky brown velvet burrowed into my neck that fateful day at the mall pet shop. Feeling impulsive and slapped silly with Cupid's arrow, every imploring gaze from his eyes locked us deeper into pet ownership. Before we knew it, we were filling out a Visa voucher and an AKC slip. The angel, Gabriel, was ours.

Our son, Nick, was still waiting in the wings to be born, and we had already decided that raising dogs was the proper precursor to raising children. We also believed that dogs should live two-by-two to keep each other company. So, Gabriel needed a wife.

Jasmine was the name of a beautiful and fragrant flower, delicate but strong. We named her months before we found her, but the movie *Aladdin* came out two months after we brought her home. Now every time someone meets her the first thing they say is, "Oh, just like Princess Jasmine!" at which I immediately leap in and explain that it had *nothing* to do with the animated character. I don't know why that bothers us so,

particularly since each of the dogs' middle names *were* inspired by Disney! (Gabriel "Triton"—Ariel's father, the Sea King, in *The Little Mermaid*—and Jasmine "Aurora"—Sleeping Beauty's real name.)

—Susan & Bill Moores

Cristina Ferrare and STAVROS, PASTA, FARFALLA & POCKET

Our first dog was a Bichon named Pastina (Pasta for short). Then we got a Maltese and named her Farfalla. In Italian, "farfalla" means butterfly. Our next dog was a purebred male mutt named Stavros. This is my husband, Tony's, dog. He originally wanted to call him Feta but we both agreed on Stavros, a good, solid Greek name. Our newest puppy is Pocket, named for the way I carry her around in my bathrobe pocket! Our daughters, Alexandra and Arianna, have two fish: Bandit, because he has black eyes, and Biscuit (go figure). And we also have a bird. I named him Diamond, because you can never have too many of those. Need I say more? That's our family of pets…and we love them all!

—Cristina Ferrare

Holly Chant & Martin Hunter and NICK

Nick is a Maine Coon cat with the registered name "Saint Cloud's Holy Terror." The "Saint Cloud's" refers to the breeder's cattery name. The "Holy Terror" is more self-explanatory. This cat loves to party, and while that doesn't exactly explain why we named him Nick, it's important background for character development. To understand the name you must first understand the cat.

Anyway, Martin and I first met on a movie called *Liebestraum*. There's a scene in the movie where the character, Sheriff Ricker, and a new guy in town walk into a bordello where my character, Maxine, works. The head "gal" in the bordello asks who this new guy is and Sheriff Ricker responds with a comical drunken intensity: "His name is Nick!"

So, after having our nameless cat for a few days, I came downstairs one morning and Martin said he had figured out what to name the kitten. He had the laser disc of *Liebestraum* cued up perfectly so that when he hit the play button, I heard Sheriff Ricker's voice bellow once again: "His name is Nick!"

—Holly Chant

Katherine Kamhi Coghlan and LIBERTY & JULY

During the Fourth of July weekend 1986, at the Statue of Liberty celebration in New York, someone handed a little orange puppy to my brother right near the statue. We fell in love with her and took her home. Of course, her name, Liberty, came pretty easily and her personality matches.

Our other dog, July, was adopted by my father from the ASPCA in New York. She was eight months old, and we couldn't think of a name for her. Since it was the month of July, and she was such a bright and cheerful dog, July seemed like the perfect name. And it still fits!

—Katherine Kamhi Coghlan

Todd Stevens and MISS PARKER

I was at a kennel and as I got out of the car, a Golden Retriever puppy ran up and started licking me. I knew right away she was "the doggy" (she was the first and last one I looked at!). She didn't have a name for two weeks. One night, some friends and I were sitting around, drinking beer, trying to think up a name for my dog. Then this girlfriend of a friend of mine said she was reading a Dorothy Parker book and suggested "Dorothy Parker." There was something about "Parker" I enjoyed, and after thinking about it for a few days, "Miss Parker" seemed to work even better. So she became Miss Parker.

And what I really like about it is in Yiddish, "mishpocheh" means "family."

—Todd Stevens

Annie Corley and FANNY

I'd had a lot of animals as a child, and I was dying to get a dog. I went to all the adoption places and finally met Fanny. She was about seven weeks old, and the woman there swore she was going to grow up to be *huge*. Well, I didn't think I could have a huge dog, so I didn't take her. But I looked and looked and two weeks later, I saw Fanny again. She had just been spayed, with little stitches on her belly, and something just told me she was the one for me. I didn't notice the fang growing out of her mouth until I brought her home and it freaked me out at first, but soon it became kind of endearing. In fact, I considered calling her "Fang," but it just didn't fit her demure personality. Since I'm a big Barbra Streisand fan, I also thought about naming the puppy after her, but I just couldn't picture myself yelling "Here, Barbara!" from across the lawn. So, I finally settled on Fanny, after her character, Fanny Brice, in *Funny Girl*. Now everyone gives me grief because together we're Annie and Fanny!

—Annie Corley

Missi, David & Miles Weinhart and ROXY & JOURNEY

One Sunday while we were shopping, I spotted a sweet, funny-looking puppy on a leash. When I went to pet her, the woman walking her explained "Sandy" was from an animal rescue group. She was found on a busy Los Angeles freeway during rush hour. Luckily a motorist managed to get the dog in her car and rush her to the animal hospital, where they treated her for mange and worms. Many different families adopted her and brought her back the next day for various reasons. I fell madly

in love with this Border Collie mix, but another family beat me to it. I was disappointed, but thankful she had finally found a home. I nearly forgot about Sandy, until the holidays came around a few weeks later—and David surprised me with her! (Once again the poor puppy had been returned.) We changed her name to Roxy, and we love her very much.

When David and I decided it was time for a second dog, we chose to adopt an animal that needed a home. We heard about a neighbor who found a male Aussie Shepherd in Oxnard, California, named Journey (because he seemed like he'd been on a long, hard journey and was unable to walk). He had been hit by a car and left with a crushed pelvis. He was also starving and dehydrated, but she nursed him back to health, and after a few months, Journey was ready for adoption. It was love at first sight when we were introduced, and Roxy loves him, too. Today he walks without a limp and even runs!

—Missi Weinhart

Hawk Koch and PEPPER

I really wanted a small female Lab, so for weeks I called the Amanda Foundation. They finally called back and said they had a seven-month-old Lab (with a little bit of Shepherd). I asked if they could bring her over, because I wanted to see if she liked my environment. But when the two women from the Amanda Foundation brought her to my house, she was really scared of me at first. I think she wasn't used to a man, and since I have a very deep voice, she was even more afraid. But her face was so expressive and I immediately wanted to keep her. Her name at the time was Jennifer, and I thought "That's a person, not a dog!" So the first night, I tried to think of a better name—something other than Susie or Julie or any other *girl's* name. Finally, since she was black, with just a hint of white, I thought of salt and pepper. And Pepper seemed like the perfect name. It's a dog's name—and yet it *can be* a girl's name—and she looks just like black pepper. She also drinks Dr. Pepper, so I'm convinced I made the right choice.

—Hawk Koch

Maritsza Lukacs and ISABELLA

My emerald green iguana, Isabella, came from El Salvador. I'm not sure why I named her Isabella—it just seemed to match her personality. I adopted her when she was one year old, but now she's five and over forty-two inches long. She's a complete vegetarian (her favorite food is strawberries), and she never leaves the cage in my backyard…at least not since the last time. I still don't know how she got out, but my heart broke when I realized she was missing. I looked all over the neighborhood, but no one had seen Isabella. It looked like she was gone for good.

Then, four days after the Northridge earthquake in January 1994, my husband looked out in the backyard—and there she was! I called out her name, and she recognized it even after being gone for nearly seven months! We put her back in her cage, and she's been with us ever since.

—Maritsza Lukacs

Jason Priestley & Christine Elise and DEMPSEY, DASHIELL, SWIFTY & FRIDAY

Our Pug, Dempsey, was our "first born." Pugs have a motto "Multum in Parvo," which means "a lot of dog in a small place." The word "pug" derives from the Latin word meaning "fight," so we decided to name our pugnacious pup Jack Dempsey—Dempsey for short. The name has special significance because my grandfather, Pat McCarthy, was a boxer and actually fought the real Jack Dempsey.

Our wolf hybrid, Dashiell, was the second to join our family. Tall, lanky, and a bit of a loner, he's reminiscent of one of my favorite writers, Dashiell Hammett. We named him in his honor.

Friday, our Pit Bull mix, was the next addition. She's sharp and quick and beautiful—like Rosalind Russell in *His Girl Friday*.

Finally, our French Bulldog, Swifty, completed the pack. Like all "Frenchies," he has this funny, "why-I-oughta..." attitude, and the name Swifty just sounded appropriate.

— *Jason Priestley*

Myra Klein and BOGART

I grew up in Chicago in a family that has had dogs for as long as I can remember. We were never without them and they were, quite simply, a part of our family. When I moved to Los Angeles, I really missed not having a pooch to come home to. So, as a way of "keeping the family connection," my mother and I decided to look for two dogs that were brothers so she could have one and so could I. We decided on Bichons because, while they're physically small, they definitely have that "big dog" personality!

My love for movies helped me choose his name—Bogart. After all, Humphrey Bogart (while a small man) did rule the silver screen for many years! My little Bogart rules the house. Everyday when I come home, he dances on his hind legs and runs speed laps around the apartment, putting on a show of his own. He makes me smile, and he is definitely one of a kind!

—Myra Klein

Mary Margaret & Fernando Martinez and SISTER B

About a year ago, a cat moved into our home. She just walked in the door and never left. That little cat made us feel like a family. We fell in love—with her, and with each other. We got married. While we were on our honeymoon…she died. Our hearts were broken, and we wondered if another cat might help mend them.

In the interim, we agreed to babysit for a friend's dog, a black-and-white Boston Terrier named Mister B. Having Mister B around reminded us how much we loved having a pet in our lives, and both of us (particularly Nando) fell in love all over again. On the day we were to return Mister B to his rightful home, we got a call from another friend asking if we knew of anyone who could give a home to a stray black-and-white female kitten crying outside his apartment. Well. We couldn't very well say no to a homeless kitty, could we? Only Nando wasn't convinced. I think he was secretly hatching a plan to kidnap Mister B. But Mister B *had* a family, and I knew this kitty needed us. And since they were both small, and black and white, I thought if I called the kitty *Sister* B, perhaps Nando would never notice.

It seems to have worked so far.

—Mary Margaret Martinez

Micky & Lori Moore and BLACK CAT

We have a black alley cat who adopted *us*. We didn't want an animal since we travel frequently, but he kept coming around, looking for food and love. We finally gave in and welcomed him into our home. He had been declawed by a family who had moved out of the neighborhood and left him to drift for himself, so how could we ignore a cat like that? He was coal black, with yellow eyes, and fur that would make a beautiful collar. But what to name him? Everyone had a suggestion, but nothing seemed to fit. Finally our eight-year-old grandson said, "How about B.C.?" We asked him what "B.C." stood for and he said, "Black Cat." We couldn't think of a more perfect name if it were staring us in the face. The funny thing is…it was!

—Micky & Lori Moore

Suzannah Galand and CHICO

In the little village of Hemel Hempstead in the heart of England, I eagerly awaited the arrival of a ruby-coated King Charles Spaniel. I was handed a rather peculiar pet with large protruding eyes that glared at me with tremendous discontent. Humored and intrigued by his offbeat appearance, I felt an insistent urge to place a cigar in his mouth—for a fleeting moment I was sure I was face to face with the ghost of Groucho Marx.

Merrily I played with my new-found friend, yelling "Groucho!" in full voice across London's Hyde Park. Besieged by onlookers who were amused by his name and all compelled to crack the old Groucho joke (the one about shooting the elephant in his pajamas), I took matters to hand and changed his name to Chico Marx. Never harassed again, we spent nine beautiful years together cherishing our moments with an abundance of humor and great love.

—Suzannah Galand

Jemma & John Wildermuth and LOLA & HANK

Our dog, Hank, was a gift to me from my husband, John. I had told him about a certain store where he could buy my birthday present, and when he went shopping, on the front door of the store was a picture of these cute Lab puppies that needed homes. John decided to get me one of the puppies for my birthday—along with another gift from the store! Since I'd always wanted to name a dog Hank (don't ask me why) the name seemed perfect for my new birthday puppy.

I got our other dog, Lola, when I was working on a movie in Douglas, Arizona on the U.S./Mexico border. During our long shoot we befriended a stray dog. Over time, she grew and grew and it was apparent she was soon going to be a new mom.

It was tough deciding who was going to get each of the new puppies—there were far more takers than there were pups! I was one of the lucky ones.

The night "Mama Stray" gave birth, several of the future parents and I were on hand to help with the delivery. When my pup was born, I decided her name was to be Lola. This pretty Spanish name seemed only appropriate for a border dog who would always remind me of the good times in that little town.

—Jemma Wildermuth

Susan Dubow and LOLA & CHAUNCEY

I bought my dog, Chauncey, on sale at Macy's in New York. He was marked down (it was a one-day sale), so I charged him on my Macy's card. The night I brought him home, he jumped on my bed…and then watched television for at least four hours straight. One of my favorite movies is *Being There,* and this little dog glued to the TV set reminded me of Peter Sellers's character in the movie. So I named him Chauncey.

I found Lola on the streets of Los Angeles many years ago, and naming her was simple: Whatever Lola wants—Lola gets.

—Susan Dubow

David Lloyd Glover & Judith Rose and MAXWELL IRVING

My name is Maxwell Irving. I'm a Schnoodle (Schnauzer/ Poodle). It took Mom and Dad forever to find just the right name for me. They called me Rover, Duke, Sydney, Alfie (as in "what's it all about?"), Murphy, King, Benji (after the movie star), Caesar, Eddie, Buster, Buddy, Mister Dog, Grover, McGillicutty (can you believe that one?), Spanky… even Spot. Then I finally heard music to my ears—Maxwell. "What a beautiful name!" I barked. "That's it! That's me!" But the decision wasn't final. Apparently Grand*paw* suggested they call me Irving. I barked loudly in protest, imagining how mortified I would be at the dog park if they yelled out, "Hey, *Irving*, come here!" But I finally agreed to a compromise— Irving became my middle name. Now every-one's happy. And when I think I could have been called Irving McGillicutty the rest of my life, I'm downright ecstatic.

—Maxwell Irving
(as dictated to David Lloyd Glover & Judith Rose)

Nancy Rosing and PUNKIN & LACEY

Where do I begin? There was a television series named *Cagney & Lacey*. My cats have always been named after someone or some significant event in my life, and since I was working on the show at the time, and since I *liked* Lacey, why not name the cat accordingly?

Lacey's about thirteen years old now, but it seems like only yesterday when I got her. I had just driven into town from Palm Springs when I got "the call" from my cousin. You know the one—"my cat had kittens," etc. She had her young daughter at the mall, at the market, trying desperately to find homes for them, and though they were cute—no takers. Would I like another cat? Well, I already had a cat, Peppermint, who might like a playmate while Mom was at work. So I got into my car and drove *another* forty-five minutes to Woodland Hills, knowing full well I'd be returning with a kitten. And sure enough—when I saw little six-week-old Lacey

and looked into those blue eyes (of course, now they're green), I said "I'll take her!"

About a year ago, Peppermint died at the age of twenty. She truly didn't want to leave me. I had been thinking about getting another kitten, but Lacey, who had always been too independent, was just beginning to be a "cuddle cat."

My sister called me one day a few months ago from the vet. "I'm holding the sweetest kitten. She's been sitting in my lap the entire time I've been here." (That was the last lap she ever sat in!) CUT TO: Nancy goes to the vet. She certainly was cute. ENTER: Punkin. She's a fiesty six-month-old who went into heat early. I had forgotten the lunacy of cats in heat! But I really fell in love with her the first night (and every night there-after) when she curled up on the pillow next to mine and started purring.

And we've lived happily ever after.

—Nancy Rosing

John Hairston & Joy Lancero and TOMMY

Tommy was originally purchased by my daughter, Tasha, who named him after the Olympic skier, Tommy Moe. Of course, the only downhill this Tommy knows is the sidewalk near our apartment where we take him on his evening walks, but his speed is just as fast as the skier's! We've only had him a short time, but we love him. He's very inquisitive, quite friendly, and even though he bugs us to play with him *constantly*, he's great company.

—John Hairston

Alan & Debbie Setlin and THOR & NATASHA

Our dog, Thor, is one of the few all-black Rottweilers I've seen. He comes from a kennel in Germany, as did his father and mother. (Thor's father was the International Grand Champion of 1993.) I named him Thor because when he barks, he sounds like the god of thunder. He's a 185-pound lap dog (or so he thinks) and he loves to cuddle.

Our American Rottweiler weighs in at about 125 pounds. Soon after we got her, we saw a Russian play in which the lead character, Natasha, struck us as very sweet and reminded us of our new Rottweiler puppy! From that moment on, Natasha was the name of our sweet-hearted Rottweiler girl. She does, occasionally, break form and kick Thor's behind once in awhile. But when he finally realizes how big he is, we're pretty sure that will stop.

—Alan Setlin

Deborah Loya and JEZZI

*J*ezzi came to our family when she was four years old. Her name is short for "Jezebel," to which she already responded when summoned for Snausages. Besides, she had originally belonged to my ex-husband's girlfriend (who seemed to be his close, personal friend long before the ink was dry on our divorce decree). Maybe I'm biased, but I think this dog's name is *perfect.*

—Deborah Loya

Ralph, Jane, Chris & Lee Jackson and BO & SASHA

Our dog, Sasha, was a birthday gift to me from my husband, Ralph and my two sons, Lee and Chris. I'm not sure why we named her Sasha—she's such a sweet, lovable dog, and it just seemed like a suitable name.

For Christmas 1990, Lee and Chris were both excited to find a new puppy. Chris finally found him at a pet store, and when we brought the pup home there was little difficulty in naming him. Both my sons played football at the time, one in high school and one at junior college. They were, and still are, very athletic and big fans of professional sports—which perfectly explains why they named the puppy Bo (his full name, of course, being Bo Jackson!). He can't play football, and he hasn't had any commercial endorsement offers yet, but *this* Bo knows how to be a great family dog.

—Jane Jackson

Steve Wilson and "ANTSCHWITZ"

Ever since I was a little lad, I loved to sit on Dad's lap and laugh with glee as we watched hard-working little ants die horribly cruel deaths under our magnifying glass. I asked my father, "Isn't the magnifying glass for studying them up close?" "Heck no," he replied, "it's for frying their sorry little asses!"

So here I am, grown up, a man dedicating his life to atone for childhood sins. I've created a home for my little ant friends called an ant farm, though it's really more of an ant "death camp." No matter how hard I try to nurture the hard-working little devils, they all die on me. I water them, I feed them, I sing them operatic ballads, but they still wind up dead. It's so sad. There they are, working day and night, industriously lifting ten times their body weight…and for what? Tunnels that lead nowhere.

Then again, it beats getting fried by a magnifying glass.

—Steve Wilson

Estelle Getty and MAZEL

A friend of mine who was living with me brought home this kitten as a Mother's Day present. He knew how much I loved cats, but I never had any because I was always worried I'd be on the road, or doing something, and I

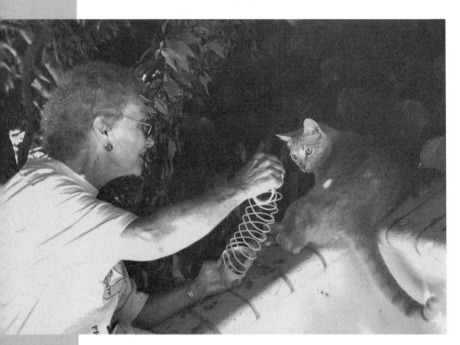

wouldn't be back at night to feed them. I told everyone, *please* don't get me anything live, not even a turtle or a goldfish. So here he shows up with this little kitten, and I was absolutely mesmerized. But I told him I would only keep the kitten for one night, and then he'd have to take him back to the shelter or wherever he got him. So the kitten stayed the night. And then another night. And then the entire week. Finally he stayed for good.

I originally thought I'd call him Leo, because he was so regal, and it's my birth sign. But then a friend of mine said, "That cat doesn't know how lucky he is—you should call him Mazel," which means "luck."

—Estelle Getty

Toti Levine and PSYMON

Thirteen years ago, a friend stopped by my apartment and dropped off a six-week-old orange kitten saying she couldn't take care of him any longer. I had just moved to L.A., had little money, no job and had always been a dog person. Cats were never part of the picture. But while I held that little kitten in my lap that day, *General Hospital* was on TV, and the psychiatrist, Dr. Simon Katz, was telling a patient to look on the bright side—things will get better. Right after that I got the phone call I'd been waiting for—I had been hired for my first television production job! In honor of the good doctor, I named my kitten Psymon Katz, and he's been the love of my life ever since!

—Toti Levine

Dweezil & Ahmet Zappa and
GODZILLA, BING JANG & ARKANSAS

Our whole family has always taken special care to invent the perfect names for our pets. Over the years we've had mostly dogs and cats, with a few birds, fish, rabbits, hamsters and raccoons thrown in for good measure.

When naming a pet, it's important to capture the animal's personality. What tends to happen at our house is very unscientific—we just throw out extremely random ideas until one sticks. Here's a list of some of the names our pets have lived with: Azzle (a male Samoyed), Doggus (a female Shepherd mix), Gorgo (a female Siamese cat), The Gweech (a female Siamese cat), Bird Reynolds (a Cockatiel), The Almighty Midnighty Black and Whitey Fighty Bitey (just Fighty Bitey for short—a female longhaired black-and-white cat), Marshmoff (a male black cat), Sourdust (a male grey-striped cat), Merfin (a female white fluffy cat), Siccootie, (a small black Shitzu), and Car Kong (a goldfish).

Our most recent beloved animal friends are Arkansas (a male Samoyed), Bing Jang (a female black Lab mix), and Godzilla. Arkansas was named because he came to us from Arkansas. Bing Jang was monikered oddly because of her hyper disposition. Her full name is Bing Jang Ding Bong (the "Ding Bong" refers to a doorbell). Bing Jang can open almost any door in our house, so I guess the name provided her with a special skill. And Godzilla because there's clearly a reptilian resemblance.

—Dweezil & Ahmet Zappa

Barbara Davis & Brigette Lester and MIA

I had a German Shepherd named Otis, and I wanted to get another one so he'd have company. I went to a pet store and saw this cute little four-week-old puppy and decided she was the one. Right away, she seemed like a daughter to me, and since "M'ija" in Spanish means "daughter," I named her Mia.

Before I got Mia I had always loved my dogs, but I never really spoiled them. That all changed with Mia. Before long, she had her own chair, her own fan, her own heater and her own radio. When we went to the market, she got her very own T-bone steak. A friend of ours came over once and saw me cooking three steaks for dinner. Thinking one was for him, he sat down at the table—then I told him, sorry, that steak's for Mia. He got up to leave and told me she ate better than he did.

I try not to spoil her so much anymore—in fact, I can't remember the last time she ate steak. But if we're in the car and she doesn't like what's on the radio or she wants to put the top down—she still always gets her way.

—Barbara Davis

David Hasselhoff and WEINER

I spent several months in Germany and Austria. While I was there, I ate a lot of "weiner schnitzel" and I noticed that everyone was walking "weiner" dogs in the park. So I bought a black Dachshund and, out of the blue, I decided to call him Weiner.

—David Hasselhoff

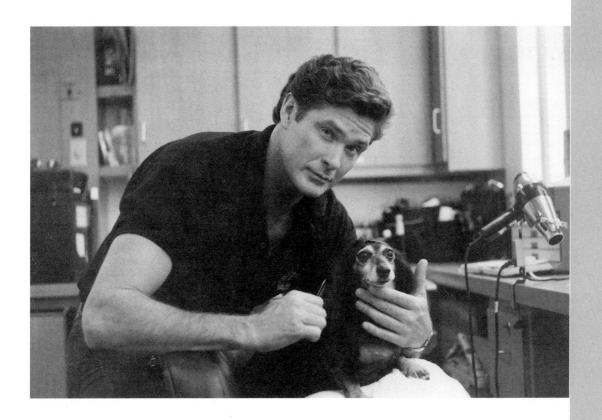

The Lawrence Brothers and JACK

We always wanted a dog, but we traveled so much it really wasn't possible to have one. We tried lower maintenance pets—an iguana, an ant hill—but they didn't really fit the bill. Finally, after seven years, Matt begged our mom and dad to get Jack. They went to a breeder's house "just to look." Of course, they immediately fell in love with the eight-week-old puppy who ran right up to them. We wanted to give him a really simple name, and on the way home Andy suggested we call him "Jack." We all liked the sound of it—so that's what we named him! His favorite pastimes are chewing our mom's underwear and goosing people.

—The Lawrence Brothers

Dot Stovall and OTIS, OPIE & DAISY

My two cats, Opie and Otis, were actually named before they came home and before I knew which sex they were. Six kittens were born to a homeless cat and I decided to give one a home. I had always been a fan of *The Andy Griffith Show* and loved the name Opie. The day before Opie came home, I found out one of the kittens still had not been claimed. What difference could another cat make? And besides, they could keep each other company. So keeping with the theme, "Otis" was put in the box along with Opie. I later found out they were both girls, but by then it was too late to name them "Aunt Bea" and "Thelma Lou." Opie was Opie and Otis was Otis, and who was I to upset Mayberry?

I had been wanting to get a dog and was looking around in shelters for that special one. After looking for a couple of weeks, I realized that a relationship with a pet is like any other—you've got to have chemistry. I would *know* when I found the right one. A friend mentioned that her neighbor had just adopted a yellow Labrador from the Guide Dogs of America and they had a few other Labs needing homes. So I decided to check them out. I walked inside the gate and this small yellow Lab ran right up to me, sat down and looked up at me with these big brown eyes, as if to say "hello." Then she jumped up to go romp with her pals. Immediately I knew she would come home with me. The rumor is that she was a kennel breeder and the owner donated her to the Guide Dogs of America, hoping they could use her in the program. If not, she would be "pushing up daisies." I couldn't resist—"Daisy" had a new name and a new home, where she now lives with Opie and Otis (who are gradually learning to accept her).

—Dot Stovall

Part II

Playing It on Your Own:

A FEW POSSIBILITIES

_T_hese names are listed in alphabetical order. I haven't grouped them, defined them, or attached explanations to them because a name may mean one thing to me, but something very different to you. The names with an asterisk next to them appeared in the first section of this book. What's important here is to get the ball rolling and jump-start your imagination!

AARON	ALDRICH	ANDREW
ABACUS	ALEC	ANDY
ABBEY	ALEX	ANGEL
ABBY	ALFRED	ANGIE
ABDUL	ALI	ANGUS
ABEL	ALICE	ANITA
ABIGAIL	ALLEGRA	ANNA
ABRAHAM	ALLISON	ANNABEL
ACE	ALMA	ANNE
ADA	ALVIN	ANNETTE
ADAM	AMADEUS	ANTHONY
ADEN	AMANDA	ANTONIA
ADMIRAL	AMAZON	ANTSCHWITZ*
ADRIAN	AMBASSADOR	APHRODITE
AFRICA	AMBER*	APPOLLONIA
AFRO	AMBROSIA	APRIL
AGATHA	AMELIA	ARCHIE
AGNES	AMI	ARKANSAS*
AJAX	AMIGO	ARNOLD
ALADDIN	AMORE	ARTHUR
ALAN	AMOS	ASHLEY*
ALBERT	AMY	ASHTON
ALBERTINA	ANASTASIA	ASPEN

ASTRO	BART	BIDDING
ATHENA	BARTHOLOMEW	BIDWELL
AUDREY	BASIL*	BIJOU
AUGUST	BAXTER	BING JANG*
AUGUSTIN	BEAR*	BIRCH
AURORA	BEATRIX	BISOU*
AUSTIN	BEAU	BISTRO
AVALON	BEAUTY	BIXBY*
AVIS	BECCA	BLACK
AVRIL	BEETHOVEN	BLACK CAT*
AZALEA	BELINDA	BLACKIE
AZZEDINE	BELL	BLACKJACK
BABE	BELLA	BLADE
BABY	BELLE*	BLAIR
BAILEY	BEN	BLANCO
BAIRD	BENEDICT	BLUE
BALDRICK	BENJI	BLUEBELLE
BALDWIN	BENNY	BO*
BALI	BENTLEY	BOB*
BALTHASAR	BERNADETTE	BOCA
BANDIT	BERNARD	BOGART*
BARBARA	BERNARDO*	BOGIE
BARBIE	BERNIE*	BOGOTA
BARNEY	BERT	BOLOGNA
BARON	BETH	BOND
BARONESS	BETTY	BONES
BARRY	BEVIS	BONNIE*

BOOMER

BOON

BOOTSIE

BOOZER

BOPPER

BORIS

BOSTON

BOSWELL

BOXER

BOYD

BRADLEY

BRANDON

BRANDY*

BRAVE

BRAVEHEART

BRAZIL

BRENDA

BREWSTER

BRIAN

BRIDGET

BRIDGITTE*

BRISTOL

BRITAIN VALEN-
  TINE*

BRITTANY

BROOK

BROWNIE

BRUCE

BRUNO

BRYONY

BUBBA

BUBBLES

BUCK

BUD

BUDDY

BUFFALO

BUFFY

BUGS

BUGSY*

BUKI*

BULLET

BUNNY

BUTCH

BUTTER
  WINDSOCK*

BUTTERCUP

BYRON

CADDY

CADILAC

CAKES

CALVIN

CAMDEN

CAMELLIA

CAMILLA

CAMPBELL

CANDY

CAPELLINI

CAPTAIN

CARI

CARL

CARLTON

CARLY

CARNEGIE

CAROL

CASHMERE

CASINO

CASPER*

CASSIDY

CASSIE*

CASTRO

CAVIAR

CECIL

CECILE

CEDRIC

CHAD

CHAMBRAY

CHANCE

CHANEL

CHANT

CHANTEL

CHAR*

CHARLES	CLARK	CORA
CHARLIE	CLEM	CORBIN
CHARLOTTE	CLEMENTINE	CORNELIA
CHAS	CLEO*	CORNELIUS
CHASE	CLEOPATRA	CORPORAL
CHAUNCEY*	CLIFFORD	COSIMA
CHELSEA	CLINT	COSMO
CHERRY	CLINTON	COUGAR*
CHERYL	CLIVE	COUNT
CHICAGO	CLOUD*	COUNTESSA
CHICO*	CLOVE	COURTNEY
CHIEF*	CLOVER	CRAIG
CHINA	CLYDE*	CRISP
CHINA ROSE	COCO	CROMWELL
CHIP	CODY	CROSBY
CHIQUITA	COLBY	CRYSTAL
CHLOE*	COLETTE	CUBA
CHLORIS	COLIN	CUPID
CHOCOLATE	COLLEEN	CURLY
CHRIS	COLONEL	CURRY
CHRISTINA	COMET	CURTIS
CHRISTINE	COMMANDER	CYRANO
CHUCK	CONAN	CYRUS
CIAO	CONRAD	DADDY
CINDERELLA	CONSTANCE	DAHLIA
CINNAMON*	COOKIE	DAISY*
CLAIRE	COPPER	DAKOTA

DALE	DENNIS	DONNA
DALLAS	DERBY	DONNER
DALTON	DERMONT	DOOGIE*
DAMIAN	DESMOND	DOOLITTLE
DAMSEL	DEUCE	DORA
DANA	DEVIL	DORIAN
DANDY	DEVON	DORIS
DANTE	DEW	DOROTHY PARKER*
DAPHNE	DEXTER	
DARCY	DIABLO	DOT
DARREN	DIANE*	DOUG
DART	DICK	DOVE
DARYL	DICKENS	DOVET
DASH	DIGBY	DRACULA
DASHIELL*	DIGGER	DRIBBLES
DAVE*	DILLINGER	DR. SEUSS*
DAVID	DILLON	DUCHESS*
DAWN	DIPPY*	DUCKY
DAZE	DIXIE	DUDE
DAZZLE	DOC	DUFF
DEENA	DODGER*	DUGAN
DEIRDRE	DOLLY	DUKE*
DELILAH	DOM	DUNCAN
DELTA	DOMINIC/K	DUNKER
DEMETRIUS	DOMINIQUE	DUSTY
DEMPSEY*	DONAHUE	DUTCH
DENISE	DONALD	DWIGHT

EARL	EMPRESS	FERNANDO
EBONY	ERIC	FERRIS
ECHO	ERNEST	FIJI
ED*	ERNESTINE	FINLAY
EDDIE*	ESPRESSO	FINN
EDGAR	ETHAN	FIONA
EDITH	ETHEL	FISK
EDMUND	EUGENE	FLAME
EDSEL	EUGENIE	FLANN
EDWARD	EUREKA	FLEUR
ELIJAH	EVA	FLINT
ELIOT	EVAN	FLIPPER
ELISE	EVE*	FLORA*
ELIZABETH TAYLOR*	EXNA	FLORENCE
ELLA	FABIAN	FLOWER*
ELLEN	FABY*	FORTUNE
ELLIOT	FAGAN	FOX
ELMO	FAITH	FOXY
ELTON	FALCON	FRAN
ELVIRA	FANNY*	FRANCES
ELVIS*	FARFALLA*	FRANK
EMERSON	FAWN	FRANKLIN
EMMA	FELICE	FRASIER
EMMET	FELICIA	FRED*
EMMY*	FELIX	FREDERICK
EMPEROR	FERGUS	FREEWAY
	FERN	FRENCHY

FRIDAY*	GERT	GUENIVERE
FRISCO	GERTY	GUMBY
FRISKI	GIGOLO	GUNNER
FRITZ	GILBERT	GUSSIE*
FROSTY	GILES	GUSTAV
GABBY	GILL	GUSTY
GABLE	GILLIAN	GUY
GABRIEL*	GINA	GWEN
GABRIELLA	GINGER	GYPSY
GALAXY	GIORGIO*	HAM
GALE	GLENN	HAMILTON
GANGSTA	GLORY	HAMLET
GARBO*	GODIVA	HANDY
GARCIA	GOGO*	HANISH
GARFIELD	GOLDIE	HANK*
GARRETT	GOMEZ*	HANNAH
GATO	GORDON	HANNIBAL
GAVIN	GOVERNOR	HAPPY
GAY	GRACE KELLY*	HARLEY*
GENERAL	GRACIE	HARLO
GENTRY	GRAHAM	HAROLD
GEOFFREY	GRANT	HARPO
GEORGE*	GREEDY	HARRIET
GEORGIA	GRETTA	HARRIS
GEORGINA	GROUCHO	HARRY
GERALD	GROVER	HART
GERALDINE	GUCCI	HAVEN

HAWK	HOLT	ISABEL
HAZARD	HOMER	ISABELLA*
HAZEL	HONEY	ISADORA
HEATHCLIFF	HOOK	ISRAEL
HEATHER	HOOVER	IVOR
HECTOR	HOPE	IVORY
HEDDA	HOUDINI	IVY
HEIDI	HOWARD	JACK*
HELEN	HOWELL	JACK STRAW
HELIOS	HOWIE*	JACOB
HELIX	HOYA*	JADE
HELOISE	HUBBELL*	JAKE
HEMINGWAY	HUCKSLEY	JAMAICA
HENLEY	HUEY	JAMES
HENRIETTA	HUGH	JAMIE
HENRY	HUGO	JANE
HEPBURN*	HUMPHREY	JASMINE*
HERBERT	HUNT	JASON
HERBIE	HUNTER	JASPER*
HERCULES	HUNTRESS	JAZZ
HERMAN	HYDE	JEFFERSON
HERMES	ICE	JEFFREY
HERO	IDA	JELLO
HILTON	IGGY*	JEMMA
HOBO	INDIA*	JENNY
HOBSON	INSPECTOR	JEROME
HOLLY	ISAAC	JERRY*

JESSICA

JESSIE*

JET

JET THE
  IGUANA PET*

JETHRO

JEWEL

JEZEBEL*

JIGGS

JILLY

JINGLES

JINX

JO

JOAN

JOANNA

JODY

JOE

JOEL

JOHN

JOKER

JONES

JORDAN

JOSEPH

JOSH

JOURNEY*

JOVE

JOY

JUDD

JUDGE

JUGS

JULIAN

JULIET

JULY*

JUNE*

JUNIOR

JUNO

JUPITER

JUSTINE

KANE

KARA

KATE

KAY

K.C. SUNSHINE
  CAT*

KEIFER

KEITH

KELLY

KENSINGTON

KENTUCKY

KENYA

KERMIT

KEVIN

KILLER

KING

KINGSTON

KIP

KIRBY

KIRK

KITTY

KIWI

KNIGHT

KNOX

KODAK

KOJAK

KOOL

KRIK

KRISTEN

KYLE

LACEY*

LADY

LADYBELLE

LADYBUG

LANCE

LANCELOT

LANDON

LARGO

LARRY

LAUREL

LAURENCE

LAVENDER

LAZY

LEA	LOGAN	MADERA
LEE	LOLA*	MADISON
LEIF	LONDON	MADONNA
LEIGH	LONNIE	MAGNOLIA
LENNOX	LORD	MAGNUM
LEO	LOTTE*	MAJOR
LEONARD	LOTUS	MAKEBA*
LEOPOLD	LOUIE*	MALCOLM
LEROY	LOUIS	MALONE
LESLIE	LOUISE	MANDELL
LEVI	LOVER	MANDY
LEWIS*	LUCAS	MANNY
LIBERTY*	LUCILLE*	MARCH
LIEUTENANT	LUCKY*	MARCO POLO
LILAC	LUCY*	MARGARET
LILIAN	LUKE*	MARGIE*
LINCOLN	LUTHER	MARGO
LINDA	LYDIA	MARIGOLD
LINK	LYNX	MARJORIE
LIONEL	MABEL	MARK
LISA	MAC	MARMALADE
LITTLE	MACARTHUR	MARTA
LITTLE FOOT*	MACHISMO	MARTIN
LIZA	MACHO	MARTINI
LIZZIE	MACK	MARY
LLOYD	MADDY	MASON
LOBO	MADELEINE	MASTER

MATILDA

MATT

MAUD

MAUI

MAURICE

MAVIS

MAX*

MAXWELL

MAXWELL
 IRVING*

MAY

MAYBELLINE*

MAYOR

MAZEL*

MECCA*

MEG

MELISSA

MEMPHIS

MERCEDES

MERLE

MIA*

MICHAEL

MICHAELA

MICK*

MICKI*

MIDAS

MIDGET

MIKE

MIKEY*

MILAN

MILES

MILLIE

MINDY

MINER

MINNESOTA

MINNIE

MINX

MIRABEL

MISSISSIPPI

MISS LUCY
 DAISY GIRL*

MISS PARKER*

MISSY

MISTER

MISTY

MOCHA

MOËT

MOLLY

MONICA

MONSTER

MONTANA

MONTGOMERY

MONTIGO

MONTY

MOON

MOOSE*

MORGAN

MOZART

MR. CAT*

MR. DESI LUCKY
 GUY*

MUFFIN

MURIEL

MURPHY

MURRAY

MUSSOLINI*

NANCY

NAPOLEON

NATALIE

NATASHA*

NED

NEIL

NELLA

NELSON

NEMESIS

NEPTUNE

NEVILLE

NEWTON

NICK*

NICKY

NIGEL

NIKE

NIKKI*

NINA

NINJA

NIPPER

NIXON

NOAH

NOBLE

NOEL

NOLA

NORA

NORDIC

NOREEN

NORMAN

NORTON*

NOVA

NUGGET*

NUTTY

ODESSA

OLE

OLIVER

OLIVIA

OLLIE

OLYMPIA

ONE FISH*

ONYX*

OPIE*

OPIUM

OPRAH

OPUS

OREO

ORLANDO

OSCAR*

OTIS*

OTTO

OUTLAW*

OWEN

OX

OZZIE*

PADDINGTON

PADDY

PAGAN

PAIGE

PALOMA

PANCHO

PANDORA

PANSY

PARIS

PASTA*

PAT

PATCHES

PATIENCE

PATRICK

PATTON

PAUL

PAULINE

PAW

PEACHES

PEARL

PEEPERS*

PENELOPE

PENNY

PEONY

PEPPER*

PERRY

PETER

PHILO

PHOEBE

PHYLLIS

P.I.

PICKLES

PILAR

PIPPA

PISTOL

PISTON

PIXIE

PLATO

POCAHANTAS

POCKET*

THE POINTER
  SISTERS*

POLLY

POLO

POMONA

POOH

POPCORN

POPPY

PORSCHE

PORTIA

POSY

POTPOURRI

POWELL

PRECIOUS*

PRETZEL

PRIMROSE

PRINCE

PRINCESS

PSYMON*

PUDDIN

PUKI

PUNKIN*

PUSSY

QUEEN

QUEENIE

QUENTIN

QUINCY

QUINN

QUIXOTE

RACHEL*

RACINE*

RADAR

RALPH

RALPHIE ROT-
TEN*

RAMONA

RAMSEY

RANDOLPH

RANDY

RAVEN

RAY

RAZZLE

REBECCA

RED

REGAN

REGGIE

RENO

REX

RHODA

RICK

RICKY

RIO*

RITA

RIVA

ROBIN

ROCKET

ROCKY

RODNEY

ROGER

ROGUE

ROJA

ROJO

ROLEX

ROLF

ROLLIN

ROLO

ROMA

ROMEO

ROMERO

ROMMEL

ROMY

ROSA

ROSCO

ROSCOE

ROSE

ROSEBUD*

ROSEMARY

ROSIE

ROUGE

ROVER

ROWAN

ROXANA

ROXY*

ROYAL

ROY THE
  IGUANA BOY*

RUBEN

RUBY*

RUDOLPH

RUDY

RUDY
  VALENTINO*

RUFFIAN

RUFUS

RUPERT

RUSSIA

RUSTY

RUTH

SABER

SABRINA

SADIE*

SAFFRON

SAHARA

SAILOR

SAINT

SALLY

SALSA

SALTY

SAM*

SAMANTHA

SAMMY DAVIS,
  JR.*

SANDRA

SANDY

SAPPHIRE

SASHA*

SASSY

SAUCY

SAVANNAH

SAWYER

SCAMP

SCARLETT

SCOOTER

SCOTCH

SCOTT

SCOUT

SCRUFFY

SEAN

SEBASTIAN

SELENA

SENATOR

SERGEANT

SERGIO

SHADOW

SHANE

SHANNON

SHARON

SHASTA

SHAUNA

SHAW

SHEBA

SHELBY

SHERLOCK

SHERRY

SHIRL

SHIRLEY

SHOOTER

SID

SIDNEY

SIENNA

SIGMUND

SILKY

SILVER

SIMON*

SINBAD

SIOUX

SISSY

SISTER B*

SKOAL

SLAM

SLICK

SLOTH

SLUGGER

SMITHFIELD
  CHRISTIAN*

SMOKEY

SNAP

SNOW

SNOWBALL

SNOWFLAKE*

SNOWY

SNUGGLES

SOJAH*

SOMBRERO

SONAR

SONNY

SOPHIE

SOX

SPANKY

SPARKY

SPECIAL

SPEEDY

SPENCER

SPHYNX

SPICE

SPIKE*

SPLASH

SPOOKY

SPOT

SPRINT

SPUD

SPUNKY*

SPY

SQUAW

SQUIRE

STACY

STAN

STANLEY

STAR

STARDUST

STARLET

STAVROS*

STELLA*

STEVE

STEWART

STORMY

STUD

STUDMUFFIN

SUGAR

SUMMER

SUMNER

SUNNY

SUSAN

SWEETIE

SWIFTY*

SYLVIE

TABBY

TABITHA*

TABOO

TAMARA

TAMSIN

TANIA

TANSY

TAOS*

TARA

TARQUIN

TATTOO

TED

TEDDY

TEENY

TEMPEST

TERESA

TERRY*

TESS

TEX*

TEXAS

THEODORA

THEODORE

THOMAS

THOR*

TIFFANY

TIGER

TILLIE*

TIM

TIMÓN	TROTSKY	VINCENT
TINA	TROUBLE	VIOLET*
TINKERBELLE	TROUPER	VIVIAN
TINY	TRUFFLES	VIXEN
TIPSY	TUBBY	VLADIMIR*
TITANIC	TUCKER*	VOODOO
TOAD	TURBO	WACKO
TOBY	TWEETY	WADDLES
TODD	TWILIGHT	WADE
TOM	TWO FISH*	WALDO
TOMASA	TYRONE	WALLABEE
TOMMY*	TYSON	WALLACE
TONI	ULF	WALLY
TONY	ULLI*	WALTER
TOPAZ	ULYSSES	WANDA
TOPSY	URSULA	WARLOCK
TOREY	VALENTINA	WARREN
TOSH	VALHALLA	WARRIOR
TOTO	VANILLA	WASHINGTON
TOY	VEGA	WATSON
TRACY*	VEGAS	WAYNE
TRAVIS	VELVET	WEBSTER*
TRENT	VERA	WEINER*
TREVOR	VERONICA*	WESEY
TRISH	VICKY	WESLEY*
TROJAN	VICTOR	WESTON
TROLL	VICTORIA	WHISKERS*

WHISKEY	WOLFGANG	ZAN
WHITE	WOODY*	ZANDRA
WICKY	WRINKLES	ZARA
WIDGET	XANADU	ZEDAK
WILBUR	XAVIER	ZEPPO
WILLOW	YALE	ZERO
WILLY	YARDLEY	ZEUS
WILSON	YASMIN	ZINNIA
WINDSOR	YETI	ZIPPY*
WINDY	YETTA	ZOE
WINKY*	YODA	ZORRO
WINNIE	YOLANDA	ZOWIE
WINSLOW	YORK	ZSA ZSA
WINSOME	YOYO	ZUKE
WINSTON	YUMA	ZULU
WOLFE	YVONNE